Mary Elizabeth Herbert

Impressions of Spain in 1866

Mary Elizabeth Herbert

Impressions of Spain in 1866

ISBN/EAN: 9783337230326

Printed in Europe, USA, Canada, Australia, Japan

Cover: Foto ©Andreas Hilbeck / pixelio.de

More available books at **www.hansebooks.com**

IMPRESSIONS OF SPAIN

IN

1866.

BY

LADY HERBERT.

WITH FIFTEEN ILLUSTRATIONS.

LONDON:

RICHARD BENTLEY, NEW BURLINGTON STREET,

Publisher in Ordinary to Her Majesty.

MDCCCLXVII.

TO

THE LADY GEORGIANA FULLERTON,

WHO HAS CONTRIBUTED

MORE THAN ANY ONE IN ENGLAND

TO GIVE A HEALTHY AND RELIGIOUS TONE TO THE

POPULAR LITERATURE OF THE DAY,

AND WHOSE WORKS ARE AN INDEX OF HER HOLY HIDDEN LIFE,

This Volume

IS AFFECTIONATELY INSCRIBED.

Oct. 26, 1866.

CONTENTS.

✦

CHAP.		PAGE
I.	ST. SEBASTIAN AND BURGOS.	1
II.	MADRID	22
III.	CORDOVA AND MALAGA	39
IV.	GRANADA	55
V.	GIBRALTAR AND CADIZ	79
VI.	SEVILLE	95
VII.	EXCURSIONS NEAR SEVILLE .	133
VIII.	THE CHARITABLE INSTITUTIONS AND CONVENTS OF SEVILLE	. 152
IX.	THE ESCURIAL AND TOLEDO	178
X.	ZARAGOSSA AND SEGOVIA	. 207
XI.	AVILA AND ALVA	227
XII.	ZAMORA AND VALLADOLID	. 248
APPENDIX		265

LIST OF ILLUSTRATIONS.

GATEWAY, BURGOS   *Frontispiece*

MADRID   *To face page*   22

MOSQUE AT CORDOVA   ,,   39

MALAGA   ..   48

ALAMEDA, CADIZ   .,   88

GIRALDA, SEVILLE   95

ALCAZAR, SEVILLE   ,.   96

GARDENS OF THE ALCAZAR   99

DOORWAY OF CATHEDRAL AT SEVILLE   ,.   116

ITALICA, SEVILLE   ,,   133

ST. THERESA STANDING FOR HER PICTURE   ,.   166

CHURCH OF LA CRUZ, TOLEDO   ,.   202

WEST DOOR OF CATHEDRAL OF AVILA   ,.   227

PALACE, GUADALAJARA   ,,   238

APOSTLES' DOOR OF CATHEDRAL, BURGOS   ,,   258

IMPRESSIONS OF SPAIN.

CHAPTER I.

ST. SEBASTIAN AND BURGOS.

WHAT is it that we seek for, we Englishmen and Englishwomen, who, year by year, about the month of November, are seen crowding the Folkestone and Dover steam-boats, with that unmistakable 'going abroad' look of travelling—bags, and wideawakes, and bundles of wraps, and alpaca gowns? I think it may be comprised in one word :—*sunshine.* This dear old land of ours, with all its luxuries, and all its comforts, and all its associations of home and people, still lacks one thing—and that is climate. For climate means health to one half of us ; and health means power of enjoyment ; for, without it, the most perfect of homes (and nowhere is that word understood so well as in England) is spoiled and saddened. So, in pursuit of this great boon, a widow lady

B

and her children, with a doctor and two other
friends, started off in the winter of 186-, in spite
of ominous warnings of revolutions, and grim
stories of brigands, for that comparatively unvisited country called Spain.   As far as St. Sebastian the journey was absolutely without interest
or adventure of any kind.   The express train
dashed them past houses and villages, and picturesque old towns with fine church towers, from
Paris to Bordeaux, and from Bordeaux to Bayonne,
and so on past the awful frontier, the scene of so
many passages-at-arms between officials and ladies'
maids, till they found themselves crossing the
picturesque bridge which leads to the little town
of St. Sebastian, with its beach of fine sand,
washed by the long billowy waves of the Atlantic
on the one hand, and its riant, well-cultivated
little Basque farms on the other.   As to the town
itself, time and the prefect may eventually make
it a second Biarritz, as in every direction lodging-
houses are springing up, till it will become what
one of Dickens' heroes would call 'the most sea-
bathingest place' that ever was !   But at present
it is a mass of rough stone and lime and scaf-
folding ; and the one straight street leading from
the hotel to the Church of S. Maria, with the
castle above, are almost all that remains of the

old town which stood so many sieges and was looked upon as the key of Northern Spain. The hotel appeared but tolerably comfortable to our travellers, fresh from the luxuries of Paris. When they returned, four or five months later, they thought it a perfect paradise of comfort and cleanliness. After wandering through the narrow streets, and walking into one or two uninteresting churches, it was resolved to climb up to the citadel which commands the town, and to which the ascent is by a fair zig-zag road, like that which leads to Dover Castle. A small garrison remains in the keep, which is also a military prison. The officers received our party very courteously, inviting them to walk on the battlements, and climb up to the flag-staff, and offering them the use of their large telescope for the view, which is certainly magnificent, especially towards the sea. There is a tiny chapel in the fortress, in which the Blessed Sacrament is reserved. It was pleasant to see the sentinel presenting arms to IT each time his round brought him past the ever open door. On the hill-side, a few monumental slabs, let in here and there into the rock, and one or two square tombs, mark the graves of the Englishmen killed during the siege, and also in the Don Carlos revolution. Of the siege itself, and

of the historical interest attached to St. Sebastian,
we will say nothing : are they not written in the
book of the chronicles of Napier and Napoleon ?

The following morning, after a fine and
crowded service at the Church of S. Maria, where
they first saw the beautiful Spanish custom of
the women being all veiled, and in black, two of
the party started at seven in the morning, in a
light carriage, for Loyola.   The road throughout
is beautiful, reminding one of the Tyrol, with
picturesque villages, old Roman bridges, quaint
manor-houses, with coats of arms emblazoned over
their porticoes ; rapid, clear trout-streams and
fine glimpses of snowy mountains on the left, and
of the bright blue sea on the right.   The flowers
too were lovely.   There was a dwarf blue bugloss
of an intensity of colour which is only equalled
by the large forget-me-not on the mountain-sides
of Lebanon.   The peasants are all small proprie-
tors.   They were cultivating their fields in the
most primitive way, father, mother, and children
working the ground with a two-pronged fork

like this : $\bigwedge$, called by them a 'laya ;' but the

result was certainly satisfactory.   They speak a
language as utterly hopeless for a foreigner to

understand as Welsh or Gaelic. The saying among
the Andalusians is, that the devil, who is no
fool, spent seven years in Bilboa studying the
Basque dialect, and learnt three words only ; and
of their pronunciation they add, that the Basque
write 'Solomon,' and pronounce it 'Nebuchad-
nezzar !' Be this as it may, they are a contented,
happy, prosperous, sober race, rarely leaving their
own country, to which they are passionately
attached, and deserving, by their independence
and self-reliance, their name of 'Bayascogara'
—'Somos bastantes.'

Passing through the baths of Certosa, the
mineral springs of which are much frequented by
the Spaniards in summer, our travellers came,
after a four hours' drive, to Azpeitia, a walled town,
with a fine church containing the 'pila,' or font,
in which St. Ignatius was baptized. Here the
good-natured curé, Padre G——, met them, and
insisted on escorting them to the great college of
Loyola, which is about a mile from the town. It
has a fine Italian façade, and is built in a fertile
valley round the house of St. Ignatius, the college
for missionary priests being on one side, and a
florid, domed, circular marble church on the other.
The whole is thoroughly Roman in its aspect,
but not so beautiful as the Gothic buildings of the

south.   They first went into the church, which is
very rich in jaspers, marbles, and mosaics, the
marbles being brought from the neighbouring
mountains.   The cloisters at the back are still
unfurnished ; but the entrance to the monastery is
of fine and good proportions, and the corridors
and staircase are very handsome.   Between the
church and the convent is a kind of covered
cloister, leading to the 'Santuario,' the actual
house in which the saint was born and lived.   The
outside is in raised brickwork, of curious old geometrical patterns ; and across the door is the
identical wooden bar which in old times served
as protection to the château.   Entering the low
door, you see on your right a staircase ; and on
your left a long low room on the ground-floor, in
which is a picture of the Blessed Virgin.   Here the
saint was born : his mother, having a particular
devotion to the Virgin, insisted on being brought
down here to be confined.   Going up the stairs,
to a kind of corridor used as a confessional, you
come first to the Chapel of St. Francis Borgia,
where he said his first mass.   Next to it is one
dedicated to Marianne di Jesu, the 'Lily of Quito,'
with a beautiful picture of the South American
saint over the high altar.   To the left again is
another chapel, and here St. François Xavier, the

Apostle of the Indies, said his mass before starting on his glorious evangelical mission. Ascending a few steps higher, their guide led them into a long low room, richly decorated and gilt, and full of pictures of the different events of the life of the saint. A gilt screen divided the ante-chapel from the altar, raised on the very spot where he lay so long with his wounded leg, and where he was inspired by the Blessed Virgin to renounce the world, and devote himself, body and soul, to the work of God. There is a representation of him in white marble under the altar as he lay; and opposite, a portrait, in his soldier's dress, said to be taken from life, and another of him afterwards, when he had become a priest. It is a beautiful face, with strong purpose and high resolve in every line of the features.

In the sacristy is the 'baldachino,' or tester of his bed, in red silk. It was in this room that he first fell sick and took to reading the Lives of the Saints to amuse himself, there being no other book within reach. Such are the 'common ways' which we blindly call 'accidents,' in which God leads those whom He chooses, like Saul, for His special service. The convent contains 30 fathers and 25 lay brothers. There are about 120 students, a fine library, refectory, &c. They have a large day-school of poor children, whom they instruct in Basque and Spanish; and distribute daily a certain number of dinners, soup, and bread, to the sick poor of the neighbouring villages, about twenty of whom were waiting at the buttery door for their daily supply.

The English strangers, taking leave of the kind and courteous fathers, had luncheon at a little 'posada' close by, where the hostess insisted on their drinking some of the cider of the country, which the doctor, himself a Devonshire man, was obliged to confess excelled that of his own country. The good curé entertained them meanwhile with stories of his people, who appear to be very like the Highlanders, both in their merits and their faults. Some of their customs seem to be derived from pagan times, such as that of offering bread and wine on the tombs of those they love on the anniversary of their death; a custom in vogue in the early days of Christianity, and mentioned by St. Augustine in his 'Confessions' as being first put a stop to by St. Ambrose, at Milan, on account of the abuses which had crept into the practice. The drive back was, if possible, even more beautiful than that of the morning, and they reached St. Sebastian at eight o'clock, delighted with their expedition.

The next day they started for Burgos, by rail, only stopping for a few minutes on their way to the station to see the 'Albergo dei Poveri,' a hospital and home for incurables, nursed by the Spanish sisters of charity. They are affiliated to the sisters of St. Vincent de Paul, and follow their rule, but do not wear the 'white cornette' of the French sisters.

The railroad in this part of Spain has been carried through most magnificent scenery, which appeared to our travellers like a mixture of Poussin and Salvator Rosa. Fine purple mountains, still sprinkled with snow, with rugged and jagged peaks standing out against the clear blue sky, and with waterfalls and beautiful streams rushing down their sides; an underwood of chesnut and beech-trees; deep valleys, with little brown villages and bright white convents perched on rising knolls, and picturesque bridges spanning the little streams as they dashed through the gorges; and then long tracks of bright rose-coloured heather, out of which rose big boulder-stones or the wayside cross; the whole forming, as it were, a succession of beautiful pictures such as would delight the heart of a painter, both as to composition and colouring. No one can say much for the pace at which the Spanish railways travel; yet

are they all too quick in scenery such as this,
when one longs to stop and sketch at every turn.
Suddenly, however, the train came to a stand-
still : an enormous fragment of rock had fallen
across the line in the night, burying a luggage-
train, but fortunately without injury to its drivers ;
and our party had no alternative but to get out,
with their manifold bags and packages, and walk
across the débris to another train, which, fortunately, was waiting for them on the opposite side
of the chasm.   A little experience of Spanish travelling taught them to expect such incidents half-
a-dozen times in the course of the day's journey ;
but at first it seemed startling and strange.   They
reached Burgos at six, and found themselves in a
small but very decent 'fonda,' where the daughter
of the landlord spoke a little French, to their
great relief. They had had visions of Italian
serving nearly as well as Spanish for making
themselves understood by the people ; but this
idea was rudely dispelled the very first day of
their arrival in Spain. Great as the similarity
may be in reading, the accent of the Spaniard
makes him utterly incomprehensible to the bewildered Italian scholar ; and the very likeness
of some words increases the difficulty when he
finds that, according to the pronunciation, a

totally different meaning is attached to them. For instance, one of the English ladies, thinking to please the mistress of the house, made a little speech to her about the beauty and cleanliness of her kitchen, using the right word (*cocina*), but pronouncing it with the Italian accent. She saw directly she had committed a blunder, though Spanish civility suppressed the laugh at her expense. She found afterwards that the word she had used, with the ' ci ' *soft*, meant a female pig. And this was only a specimen of mistakes hourly committed by all who adventured themselves in this unknown tongue.

A letter of introduction procured for our travellers an instant admission to the Cardinal Archbishop, who received them most kindly, and volunteered to be their escort over the cathedral. He had been educated at Ushaw, and spoke English fluently and well. He had a very pretty little chapel in his palace, with a picture in it of Sta. Maria della Pace at Rome, from whence he derives his cardinal's title.

The cathedral at Burgos, with the exception of Toledo, is the most beautiful Gothic building in Spain. It was begun by Bishop Maurice, an Englishman, and a great friend of St. Ferdinand's, in the year 1220. The spires, with their lacework

carving; the doorways, so rich in sculpture; the
rose-windows, with their exquisite tracery; the
beautiful lantern-shaped clerestory; the curious
double staircase of Diego de Siloe; the wonderful 'retablos' behind the altars, of the finest
wood-carving; the magnificent marble and alabaster monuments in the side chapels, vying with
one another in beauty and richness of detail; the
wonderful wood-carving of the stalls in the choir;
the bas-reliefs carved in every portion of the
stone; in fact, every detail of this glorious building is equally perfect; and even in Southern
Spain, that paradise for lovers of cathedrals, can
scarcely be surpassed. The finest of the monuments are those of the Velasco family, the here-
ditary high-constable of Castile. They are of
Carrara marble, resting upon blocks of jasper:
at the feet of the lady lies a little dog, as the
emblem of 'Fidelity.' Over the doorway of
this chapel, leading to a tiny sacristy, are carved
the arms of Jerusalem. In the large sacristy is
a Magdalen, by Leonardo da Vinci; and some
exquisite church plate, in gold and enamel, especially a chalice, a processional cross, a pax, &c.
In the first chapel on the right, as you enter by
the west door, is a very curious figure of Christ,
brought from the Holy Land, with real hair and

skin; but painful in the extreme, and almost grotesque from the manner in which it has been dressed. This remark, however, applies to almost all the images of Christ and of the Blessed Virgin throughout Spain, which are rendered both sad and ludicrous to English eyes from the petticoats and finery with which modern devotion has disfigured them. This crucifix, however, is greatly venerated by the people, who call it 'The Christ of Burgos,' and on Sundays or holidays there is no possibility of getting near it, on account of the crowd. In the Chapel of the Visitation are three more beautiful monuments, and a very fine picture of the Virgin and Child, by Sebastian del Piombo. But it was impossible to take in every portion of this cathedral at once; and so our travellers went on to the cloisters, passing through a beautiful pointed doorway, richly carved, which leads to the chapter-house, now a receptacle for lumber, but containing the chest of the Cid, regarding which the old chronicle says: 'He filled it with sand, and then, telling the Jews it contained gold, raised money on the security.' In justice to the hero, however, we are bound to add, that when the necessities of the war were over, he repaid both principal and interest. Leaving, at last, the cloisters and cathedral, and taking leave of the

kind archbishop, our party drove to the Town
Hall, where, in a walnut-wood urn, are kept the
bones of the Cid, which were removed twenty
years ago from their original resting-place at
Cardena. The sight of them strengthened their
resolve to make a pilgrimage to his real tomb,
which is in a Benedictine convent about eight
miles from the town. Starting, therefore, in two
primitive little carriages, guiltless of springs,
they crossed the river and wound up a steep hill
till they came in sight of *Miraflores*, the great
Carthusian convent, which, seen from a distance,
strongly resembles Eton College Chapel. It was
built by John II. for a royal burial-place, and
was finished by Isabella of Castile. Arriving at
the monastery, from whence the monks have been
expelled, and which is now tenanted by only one
or two lay brothers of the Order, they passed
through a long cloister, shaded by fine cypresses,
into the church, in the chancel of which is that
which may really be called one of the seven wonders of the world. This is the alabaster sepulchre
of John II. and his wife, the father and mother
of Queen Isabella, with their son, the Infante
Alonso, who died young. In richness of detail,
delicacy of carving, and beauty of execution, the
work of these monuments is perfectly unrivalled—

the very material seems to be changed into Mechlin lace. The artist was Maestro Gil, the father of the famous Diego de Siloe, who carved the staircase in the cathedral. He finished it in 1493 ; and one does not wonder at Philip II.'s exclamation when he saw it : ' *We* have done nothing at the Escurial.' In the sacristy is a wonderful statue of St. Bruno, carved in wood, and so beautiful and life-like in expression, that it was difficult to look at anything else.

Leaving Miraflores, our travellers broke tenderly to their coachmen their wish to go on to Cardena. One of them utterly refused, saying the road was impassable ; the other, *moyennant* an extra gratuity, undertook to try it, but stipulated that the gentleman should walk, and the ladies do the same, if necessary. Winding round the convent garden walls, and then across a bleak wild moor, they started, and soon found themselves involved in a succession of ruts and Sloughs of Despond which more than justified the hesitation of their driver. On the coach-box was an imp of a boy, whose delight consisted in quickening the fears of the most timid among the ladies by invariably making the horses gallop at the most difficult and precipitous parts of the road, and then turning round and grinning at the fright he had given them. It is needless to say that the carriage was not his property. At last, the horses came to a stand-still; they could go no farther, and the rest of the way had to be done on foot. But our travellers were not to be pitied; for the day was lovely, and the path across the moor was studded with flowers. At last, on climbing over a steep hill which had intercepted their view, they came on a lovely panorama, with a background of blue mountains tipped with snow; a wooded glen, in which the brown convent nestled, and a wild moor foreground, across which long strings of mules with gay trappings, driven by peasants in Spanish costumes, exactly as represented in Ansdell's paintings, were wending their way towards the city. Tired as some of our party were, this glorious view seemed to give them fresh strength, and they rapidly descended the hill by the hollow path leading to the convent. Over the great entrance is a statue of the Cid, mounted on his favourite horse, 'Babieca,' who bore him to his last resting-place, and was afterwards buried beside the master he loved so well. But the grand old building seemed utterly deserted, and a big mastiff, fastened by an ominously slight chain to the doorway, appeared determined to defy their attempts to enter. At last, one of them, more courageous than the rest, tempting the Cerberus with the remains of her luncheon, got past him, and wandered through the cloister, up a fine staircase to a spacious corridor, in hopes of finding a guide to show them the way to the chapel, where lay the object of their expedition, i.e., the monument of the Cid. But she was only answered by the echo of her own footsteps. The cells were empty ; the once beautiful library gutted and destroyed ; the refectory had nothing in it but bare walls—the whole place was like a city of the dead. At last, she discovered a staircase leading down to a cloister on the side opposite the great entrance, and there a low-arched door, which she found ajar, admitted her into the deserted church. The tomb of the Cid has been removed from the high altar to a side chapel ; and there is interred, likewise, his faithful and devoted wife Ximena, and their two daughters. On his shield is emblazoned the ' tizona,' or sparkling brand, which the legends affirm he always carried in his hand, and with which he struck terror into the hearts of the infidels. This church and convent, built for the Benedictines by the Princess Sancho, in memory of her son Theodoric, who was killed out hunting, was sacked by the Moors in the ninth century, when 200 of the monks were murdered. A tablet

c

in the south transept still remains, recording the
massacre; but the monument of Theodoric has
been mutilated and destroyed. The Christian
spoilers have done their work more effectually
than the Moslem! Sorrowfully our travellers left
this beautiful spot, thinking bitterly on the so-
called age of progress which had left the abode
of so much learning and piety to the owls and
the bats; and partly walking, partly driving, returned without accident to the city. One more
memento of the Cid at Burgos deserves mention.
It is the lock on which he compelled the king,
Alonso VI., to swear that he had had no part in
his brother Sancho's assassination at Zamora. All
who wished to confirm their word with a solemn
oath used to touch it, till the practice was abolished by Isabella, and the lock itself hung up in
the old Church of St. Gadea, on the way to the
Castle Hill, where it still rests. This is the origin
of the peasant. custom of closing the hand and
raising the thumb, which they kiss in token of
asseveration; and in like manner we have the old
Highland saying : ' There's my thumb. I'll not
betray you.'

Another charming expedition was made on
the following day to Las Huelgas, the famous
Cistercian nunnery, built in some gardens outside

the town by Alonso VIII. and his wife Leonora, daughter of our king Henry II.

When one of the ladies had asked the cardinal for a note of introduction to the abbess, he had replied, laughing : 'I am afraid it would not be of much use to you. She certainly is not under my jurisdiction, and I am not sure whether she does not think I am under hers!' No lady abbess certainly ever had more extraordinary privileges. She is a Princess Palatine—styled 'by the Grace of God'—and has feudal power over all the lands and villages round. She appoints her own priests and confessors, and has a hospital about a mile from the convent, nursed by the sisters, and entirely under her control. After some little delay at the porter's lodge, owing to their having come at the inconvenient hour of dinner, our party were ushered into the parlour, and there, behind a grille, saw a beautiful old lady, dressed in wimple and coif, exactly like a picture in the time of Chaucer. This was the redoubtable lady abbess. There are twenty-seven choir nuns and twenty-five lay sisters in the convent, and they follow the rule of St. Bernard. The abbess first showed them the Moorish standard, beautifully embroidered, taken at the battle of Las Navas de Tolosa, in 1180. A curious old fresco representing this battle remains over the arch of the church. She then took them to the choir, which is very rich in carving, and contains the tombs of the founders, Alonso and Leonora, and also of a number of Infantas, whose royal bodies are placed in richly carved Gothic sepulchres, resting on lions, on each side of the choir. In the church is a curious hammered iron gilt pulpit, in which St. Vincent de Ferrer preached. Here St. Ferdinand and Alonso XI. knighted themselves, and here our own king, Edward I., received the honour of knighthood at the hands of Alonso el Sabio.

The church is a curious jumble of different dates of architecture ; but there is a beautiful tower and doorway, some very interesting old monuments, and a fine double rose-window. The cloisters are very beautiful, with round-headed arches, grouped pillars, and Norman capitals. The lady abbess then ordered one of the priests of the convent to take her English visitors to see their hospital, called 'Del Rey,' the walk to which from the convent is through pleasant fields like English meadows. It is admirably managed and nursed by the nuns. Each patient has a bed in a recess, which makes, as it were, a little private room for each, and this is lined with 'azulejos,' or coloured

tiles, up to a certain height, giving that clean
bright look which distinguishes the Spanish hospitals from all others.   At the end of each ward
was a little altar, where mass is daily performed
for the sick.   There are fifty men and fifty women,
and the surgical department was carefully supplied with all the best and newest instruments,
which the surgeon was eager to show off to the
doctor, the only one of the party worthy of the
privilege.   The wards opened into a 'patio,' or
court, with seats and bright flowers, where the
patients who could leave their beds were sitting
out and sunning themselves.   Altogether, it is a
noble institution; and one must hope that the
ruthless hand of government will not destroy it
in common with the other charitable foundations
of Spain.

CHAPTER II.

MADRID.

BUT the cold winds blew sharply, and our travellers resolved to hurry south, and reserve the further treasures of Burgos for inspection on their return. The night train conveyed them safely to Madrid, where they found a most comfortable hotel in the ' Ville de Paris,' lately opened by an enterprising Frenchman, in the ' Puerta del Sol ; ' and received the kindest of welcomes from the English minister, the Count T. D., and other old friends. It was Sunday morning, and the first object was to find a church near at hand. These are not wanting in Madrid, but all are modern, and few in good taste : the nicest and best served is undoubtedly that of ' St. Louis des Français,' though the approach to it through the crowded market is rather disagreeable early in the morning. The witty writer of ' Les Lettres d'Espagne ' says truly : ' Madrid *ne me dit rien* : c'est moderne, aligné, propre et civilisé.' As for the climate, it

is detestable : bitterly cold in winter, the east wind searching out every rheumatic joint in one's frame, and pitilessly driving round the corners of every street ; burning hot in summer, with a glare and dust which nearly equal that of Cairo in a simoom.

The Gallery, however, compensates for all. Our travellers had spent months at Florence, at Rome, at Dresden, and fancied that nothing could come up to the Pitti, the Uffizi, or the Vatican—that no picture could equal the 'San Sisto ; ' but they found they had yet much to learn. No one who has not been in Spain can so much as imagine what Murillo is. In England, he is looked upon as the clever painter of picturesque brown beggar-boys : there is not one of these subjects to be found in Spain, from St. Sebastian to Gibraltar ! At Madrid, at Cadiz, but especially at Seville, one learns to know him as he is—i. e. the great mystical religious painter of the seventeenth century, embodying in his wonderful conceptions all that is most sublime and ecstatic in devotion, and in the representation of Divine love. The English minister, speaking of this one day to a lady of the party, explained it very simply, by saying that the English generally only carried off those of his works in which the Catholic feeling was not so strongly displayed. It would be hopeless to attempt to describe all his pictures in the Madrid Gallery. The Saviour and St. John, as boys, drinking out of a shell, is perhaps the most delicate and exquisite in colouring and expression; but the 'Conception' surpasses all. No one should compare it with the Louvre pictures of the same subject. There is a refinement, a tenderness, and a beauty in the Madrid 'Conception' entirely wanting in the one stolen by the French. Then there is Velasquez, with his inimitable portraits; full of droll originality, as the 'Æsop;' or of deep historical interest, as his 'Philip IV.;' or of sublime piety, as in his 'Crucifixion,' with the hair falling over one side of the Saviour's face, which the pierced and fastened hands cannot push aside: each and all are priceless treasures, and there must be sixty or seventy in that one long room. Ford says that 'Velasquez is the Homer of the Spanish school, of which Murillo is the Virgil.' Then there are Riberas, and Zurbarans, Divino Morales, Juan Joanes, Alonso Caño, and half-a-dozen other artists, whose very names are scarcely known out of Spain, and all of whose works are impregnated with that mystic, devotional, self-sacrificing spirit which is the essence of Catholicism. The Italian school is equally magnificently represented. There are exquisite Raphaels, one especially, 'La Perla,' once belonging to our Charles I., and sold by the Puritans to the Spanish king; the 'Spasimo,' the 'Vergin del Pesce,' &c.; beautiful Titians, not only portraits, but one, a 'Magdalen,' which is unknown to us by engravings or photographs in England, where, in a green robe, she is flying from the assaults of the devil, represented by a monstrous dragon, and in which the drawing is as wonderful as the colouring; beautiful G. Bellinis, and Luinis, and Andrea del Sartos (especially one of his wife), and Paul Veronese, and others of the Venetian and Milanese schools. In a lower room there are Dutch and Flemish chefs-d'œuvre without end: Rubens, and Vandyke, and Teniers, and Breughel, and Holbein, and the rest. It is a gallery bewildering from the number of its pictures, but with the rare merit of almost all being good; and they are so arranged that the visitor can see them with perfect comfort at any hour of the day. In the ante-room to the long gallery are some pictures of the present century, but none are worth looking at save Goya's pictures of the wholesale massacre of the Spanish prisoners by the French, which are not likely to soften the public feeling of bitterness and hostility towards that nation.

There is nothing very good in sculpture, only
two of the antiques being worth looking at ; but
there is a fine statue of Charles V., and a wonderfully beautiful St. John of God, carrying a sick
man out of the burning hospital on his back,
which is modern, but in admirable taste. Neglected, in some side cupboards, and several of them
broken and covered with dust and dirt, are some
exquisite tazzas of Benvenuto Cellini, D'Arphes,
and Beceriles, in lapis, jade, agate, and enamel,
finer than any to be seen even in the Grüne Ge-
wölbe of Dresden. There is a gold mermaid,
studded with rubies, and with an emerald tail, and
a cup with an enamelled jewelled border and
stand, which are perfectly unrivalled in beauty of
workmanship. Then, in addition to this matchless gallery, Madrid has its 'Academia,' containing three of Murillo's most magnificent conceptions. One is 'St. Elizabeth of Hungary,' washing the wounds of the sick, her fair young face
and delicate white hands forming a beautiful
contrast with the shrivelled brown old woman in
the foreground. The expression of the saint's
countenance is that of one absorbed in her work
and yet looking beyond it.* The other is the

* This picture was stolen from the Caridad, at Seville, by the
French, and afterwards sent back to Madrid, where it still remains.

'Dream,' in which the Blessed Virgin appears to the founder of the Church of S. Maria della Neve (afterwards called S. Maria Maggiore) and his wife, and suggests to them the building of a church on a spot at Rome, which would be indicated to them by a fall of snow, though it was then in the month of August. In the third picture the founder and his wife are kneeling at the feet of the Pope, telling him of their vision, and imploring his benediction on their work. These two famous pictures were taken by Soult from Seville, and are of a lunette shape, being made to fit the original niche for which they were painted : both are unequalled for beauty of colour and design, and have recently been magnificently engraved, by order of the government.

But apart from its galleries, Madrid is a disappointment ; there is no antiquity or interest attached to any of its churches or public buildings. The daily afternoon diversion is the drive on the Prado ; amusing from the crowd, perhaps, but where, with the exception of the nurses, all national costume has disappeared. There are scarcely any mantillas; but Faubourg St.-Germain bonnets, in badly assorted colours, and horrible and exaggerated crinolines, replacing the soft, black, flowing dresses of the south. It is, in fact, a bad *réchauffé* of the Bois de Boulogne. The queen, in a carriage drawn by six or eight mules, surrounded by her escort, and announced by trumpeters, and the infantas, following in similar carriages, form the only ' event ' of the afternoon. Poor lady ! how heartily sick she must be of this promenade ! She is far more pleasing-looking than her pictures give her credit for, and has a frank kind manner which is an indication of her good and simple nature. Her children are most carefully brought up, and very well educated by the charming English authoress, Madame Calderon de la Barca, well known by her interesting work on Mexico. On Saturdays, the queen and the royal family always drive to Atocha, a church at the extreme end of the Prado, in vile taste, but containing the famous image of the Virgin, the patroness of Spain, to whom all the royalties are specially devoted. It is a black image, but almost invisible from the gorgeous jewels and dresses with which it is adorned.

One of the shows of Madrid is the royal stables, which are well worth a visit. There are upwards of 250 horses, and 200 fine mules ; the backs of the latter are invariably shaved down to a certain point, which gives them an uncomfortable appearance to English eyes, but is the custom throughout Spain. One lady writer asserts that

' it is more modest ! ' There is a charming little stud belonging to the Prince Imperial, which includes two tiny mules not bigger than dogs, but in perfect proportions, about the size required to drag a perambulator. Some of the horses are English and thoroughbred, but a good many are of the heavy-crested Velasquez type. The carriages are of every date, and very curious. Among them is one in which Philip I. (le Bel) was said to have been poisoned, and in which his wife, Jeanne la Folle, still insisted on dragging him out, believing he was only asleep.

More interesting to some of our party than horses and stables were the charitable institutions in Madrid, which are admirable and very numerous. It was on the 12th of November, 1856, that the Mère Dévos, afterwards Mère Générale of the Order of St. Vincent de Paul, started with four or five of her sisters of charity to establish their first house in Madrid. They had many hardships and difficulties to encounter, but loving perseverance conquered them all. The sisters now number between forty and fifty, distributed in three houses in different parts of the city, with more than 1,000 children in their schools and orphanages, the whole being under the superintendence of the Sœur Gottofrey, the able and charming French

' provincial ' of Spain. The queen takes a lively interest in their success, and most of the ladies of her court are more or less affiliated to them. There are branch houses of these French sisters at Malaga, Granada, Barcelona, and other towns ; and they are now beginning to undertake district visiting, as well as the care of the sick and the education of children—a proceeding which they were obliged to adopt with caution, owing to the strong prejudice felt in Spain towards any religious orders being seen outside their ' clausura,' and also towards their dress, the white cornette, which, to eyes unaccustomed to anything but black veils, appeared outrageous and unsuitable. The Spanish sisters of charity, though affiliated to them, following the rule of St. Vincent, and acknowledging N. T. H. Père Étienne as their superior, still refuse to wear the cornette, and substitute a simple white cap and black veil. These Spanish sisters have the charge of the magnificent Foundling Hospital, which receives upwards of 1,000 children ; of the hospital called Las Recogidas, for penitents ; of the General Hospital, where the sick are admirably cared for, and to which is attached a wing for patients of an upper class, who pay a small sum weekly, and have all the advantages of the clever surgery and careful nursing of the hospital (an

arrangement sadly needed in our English hospitals) ; of the Hospicio de S. Maria del Cármen,
founded by private charity, for the old and incurables ; of the infant school, or ' salle d'asile,' where
the children are fed as well as taught ; and of the
Albergo dei Poveri, equivalent to what we should
call a workhouse in England, but which we cannot
desecrate by such a name when speaking of an establishment conducted on the highest and noblest
rules of Christian charity, and where the orphans
find not only loving care and tender watchfulness,
but admirable industrial training, fitting them
to fill worthily any employments to which their
natural inclination may lead them. The Sacré
Cœur have a large establishment for the education
of the upper classes at Chaumartin de la Rosa, a
suburb of Madrid, about four miles from the town.
It was founded by the Marquesa de Villa Nueva, a
most saint-like person, whose house adjoins, and
in fact forms part of, the convent—her bedroom
leading into a tribune overlooking the chapel and
the Blessed Sacrament. The view from the large
garden, with the mountains on the one hand, and
the stone pine woods on the other, is very pretty,
and unlike anything else in the neighbourhood of
Madrid. The superior, a charming person, showed
the ladies all over the house, which is large,

commodious, and airy, and in which they have already upwards of eighty pupils. They have a very pretty chapel, and in the parlour a very beautiful picture of St. Elizabeth, by a modern artist.

One more 'lion' was visited before leaving Madrid, and that was the Armoury, which is indeed well worth a long and careful examination. The objects it contains are all of deep historical interest. There is a collar-piece belonging to Philip II., with scenes from the battle of St. Quentin exquisitely carved; a helmet taken from the unfortunate Boabdil, the last Moorish king of Granada; beautiful Moorish arms and Turkish banners taken at the battle of Lepanto, in old Damascus inlaid-work; the swords of Boabdil, and of Ferdinand and Isabella; the armour of the Cid, of Christopher Columbus, of Charles V., of St. Ferdinand, and of Philip II.; the carriage of Charles V., looking like a large bassinet; exquisite shields, rapiers, swords, and helmets; some very curious gold ornaments, votive crowns, and crosses of the seventh century; and heaps of other treasures too numerous to be here detailed. But our travellers were fairly exhausted by their previous sight-seeing, and gladly reserved their examination of the rest to a future day. At all times, a *return* to a place is more interesting

than a first visit; for in the latter, one is op-
pressed by the feeling of the quantity to be seen
and the short time there is to see it in, and so the
intense anxiety and fatigue destroy half one's enjoyment of the objects themselves. That evening
they were to leave the biting east winds of Madrid
for the more genial climate of sunny Malaga; and
so, having made sundry very necessary purchases,
including mantillas and chocolate, and having
eaten what turned out to be their last good dinner for a very long time, they started off by an
eight o'clock train for Cordova, which was to be
their halting-place midway. On reaching Alcazar,
about one o'clock in the morning, they had to
change trains, as the one in which they were
branched off to Valencia; and for two hours they
were kept waiting for the Cordova train. Oh! the
misery of those wayside stations in Spain! One
long low room filled with smokers and passengers
of every class, struggling for chocolate. served in
dirty cups by uncivil waiters, with insufficient seats
and scant courtesy : no wonder that the Spaniards
consider our waiting-rooms real palaces. You have
no alternative in the winter season but to endure
this fœtid, stifling atmosphere, and be blinded
with smoke, or else to freeze and shiver outside,
where there are no benches at all, and your only

hope is to get a corner of a wall against which you can lean and be sheltered from the bitter wind. The arrival of the up train brought, therefore, unmixed joy to our party, who managed to secure a compartment to themselves without any smokers (a rare privilege in Spain), and thus got some sleep for a few hours. At six o'clock the train stopped, the railroad went no farther; so the passengers turned out somewhat ruefully in the cold, and gazed with dismay at the lumbering dirty diligences, looking as if they had come out of the Ark, which were drawn up, all in a row, at the station door, with ten, twelve, or fourteen mules harnessed to each, and by which they and their luggage were to be conveyed for the next eight hours. The station-master was a Frenchman, and with great civility, during the lading of the diligences, gave up to the ladies his own tiny bedroom and some fresh water to wash themselves a little and make themselves comfortable after their long night journey, for there was no pretence of a waiting-room at this station.

Reader, did you ever go in a Spanish diligence? It was the first experience of most of our party of this means of locomotion, and at first seemed simply impossible. The excessive lowness of the carriages, the way in which the unhappy passen-

gers are jammed in, either into the *coupé* in front,
or into the square box behind, unable to move or
sit upright in either; while the mules plunge
and start off in every direction but the right one,
their drivers every instant jumping down and
running by the side of the poor beasts, which
they flog unmercifully, vociferating in every key;
and that, not at first starting, but all the way, up
hill and down dale, with an energy which is as
inexhaustible as it is despairing, till either a pole
cracks, or a trace breaks, or some accident happens to a wheel, and the whole lumbering con-
cern stops with a jerk and a lurch which threaten
to roll everything and everybody into the gorge
below. Each diligence is accompanied by a 'mayoral,' or conductor, who has charge of the whole
equipage, and is a-very important personage.
This functionary is generally gorgeously dressed,
with embroidered jacket, scarlet sash round the
waist, gaiters with silver buttons and hanging
leather strips, and round his head a gay-coloured
handkerchief and a round black felt hat with
broad brim and feather, or else of the kind deno-
minated 'pork pie' in England; he is here, there,
and everywhere during the journey, arranging the
places of the passengers, the stations for halts, and
the like. Besides this dignitary, there is the 'moto'

or driver, whose business is to be perpetually jumping down and flogging the far-off mules into a trot,
which he did with such cruelty that our travellers
often hoped he would himself get into trouble in
jumping up again, which, unfortunately, he was
always too expert to do.   Every mule has its
name, and answers to it.   They are harnessed two
abreast, a small boy riding on the leaders; and it
is on his presence of mind and skill that the guidance and safety of the whole team depend.   On
this occasion, the 'mayoral' and 'moto' leant
with their backs against what was left of the windows of the *coupé*, which they instantly smashed,
the cold wind rushed in, and the passengers were
alternately splashed from head to foot with the
mud cast up in their faces by the mules' heels,
or choked and blinded with dust.   For neither
misfortune is there either redress or sympathy.
The lower panels of the floor and doors have
holes cut in them to let out the water and
mud; but the same agreeable arrangement, in
winter, lets in a wind which threatens to freeze
off your feet as you sit.   A small boy, who, it
is to be supposed, was learning his trade, held
on by his eyelids to a ledge below, and was
perpetually assisting in screaming and flogging.
A struggle at some kind of vain resistance,

and then a sullen despair and a final making up one's mind that, after all, it can't last for ever, are the phases through which the unhappy travellers pass during these agreeable diligence journeys. It was some little time before our party could get sufficiently reconciled to their misery to enjoy the scenery. But when they could look about them, they found themselves passing through a beautiful gorge, and up a zig-zag road, like the lower spurs of an Alpine pass, over the Sierra Morena. Then began the descent, during which some of the ladies held their breath, expecting to be dashed over the parapet at each sharp turn in the road: the pace of the mules was never relaxed, and the unwieldy top-heavy mass oscillated over the precipice below in a decidedly unpleasant manner. Then they came into a fertile region of olives and aloes, and so on by divers villages and through roads which the late rains had made almost impassable, and in passing over which every bone of their bodies seemed dislocated in their springless vehicle, till, at two o'clock in the afternoon, they reached the station, where, to their intense relief, they again came upon a rail-road. Hastily swallowing some doubtful chocolate, they established themselves once more comfortably in the railway carriage ; but after being in the enjoyment of this luxury for half an hour, the train came, all of a sudden, to a stand-still ; and the doors being opened, they were politely told that they must *walk*, as a landslip had destroyed the line for some distance. Coming at last to a picturesque town with a fine bridge over the Guadalquiver, they were allowed once more to take their seats in the carriages, and finally arrived at Cordova at eight o'clock at night, after twenty-four hours of travelling, alternating from intense cold to intense heat, very tired indeed, horribly dusty and dirty, and without having had any church all day.

Mosque at Cordova.

CHAPTER III.

CORDOVA AND MALAGA.

A COMFORTABLE little old-fashioned inn, with a
'patio' full of orange-trees, leading to a public
'sala,' rather like a room at Damascus, with
alcoves and fountains, gladdened the hearts of our
wearied travellers. After a good night's rest (and
one advantage in Spain is, that except mosqui-
toes, your beds are generally free from other inhabitants), they started down the narrow, badly-
paved streets to visit the cathedral. The exterior
is disappointing, as all you see is a buttressed
wall, with square towers sixty feet high, opposite
which is the gateway and wall of the archiepiscopal
palace. But on passing through a low arched door,
you come into a beautiful Oriental court, in the
centre of which is a picturesque Moorish fountain,
the rest of the space being filled with orange-
trees and palms, and on the north side an exquisite giralda, or tower, from whence there is a

beautiful view over the whole town and neighbourhood. All the entrances to the mosque (now the cathedral) from this court are closed, except the centre one. Entering by that, a whole forest of pillars bursts upon you, with horse-shoe arches interlacing one another, and forming altogether the most wonderful building in the world. The Moors collected these pillars, of which there are upwards of a thousand, from the temples of Carthage, of Nismes, and of Rome, and adapted them to their mosque. Some are of jasper, some of verde-antique, some of porphyry—no two are alike. The pillars have no plinths, and divide the mosque into nineteen longitudinal and twenty-nine transverse aisles ; hence the immense variety and beauty of the intersection of the arches. This mosque was built in the eighth century, and ranked in sanctity with the ' Alaksa ' of Jerusalem and the ' Caaba ' of Mecca.

A pilgrimage to it was, indeed, considered equivalent to that of Mecca, and hence the Spanish proverb to express distant wanderings, ' Andar de zeca en Meca.' The roof is of arbor vitæ, and is in perfect preservation. Two of the moresque chapels are exquisite in carving and richness of detail, one being that of the Caliphs, and the other the ' Holy of Holies,' where the

Koran was kept. The beauty and delicacy of the moresque work, with its gold enamel and lovely trefoiled patterns, its quaint lions and bright-coloured 'azulejos' (tiles), exceeds anything of the sort in Europe. The roof is in the form of a shell, and exquisitely wrought out of one single piece of marble. The mosaic border was sent to Cordova by Romanus II., from Constantinople. When the brother of the king of Morocco came there a year or two ago, he went round this 'Holy of Holies' seven times on his knees, crying bitterly all the time. The inscriptions in this mosque are in Cufic, and not in Arabic. The whole carries one back to Damascus and the East in a way which makes it difficult to realise that one is still in Europe. The choir is a horrible modern 'churri-queresque' innovation, stuck in the centre of the beautiful forest of Saracenic columns, many of which were destroyed to make room for it. Even Charles V. protested against the bad taste of the chapter when he saw it completed in 1526, and exclaimed: 'You have built a thing which one can see anywhere ; and to do so, you have destroyed what was unique in the world.' The carving of the choir is certainly fine, but the incongruity of the whole jars on one's taste too keenly for any kind of admiration. The only beautiful and solemn modernised portion of the building is the chapel of the cardinal, with fine tombs and a deep recess for the Blessed Sacrament, with a magnificent silver tabernacle. From the cathedral, some of the party went to visit the bishop, who received them very kindly, and sent his secretary to show them the treasures of the cathedral. The 'custodia,' of the fifteenth century, is in silver-gilt, with beautiful emeralds, and exquisitely carved; it is the work of Arphe, the Benvenuto Cellini of Spain. There are also some beautiful processional crosses, reliquaries, chalices, and pax, secreted at the time of Dupont's French invasion, and so saved from the universal plunder.

Having spent the morning in the cathedral, our travellers wandered down to the fine Roman bridge, of sixteen arches, over the Guadalquiver, looking upon some picturesque Moorish mills and orange gardens. To the left is a statue of St. Raphael, the guardian angel of Cordova; and close by is the Alcazar, now a ruin, formerly the palace of Roderick, the last of the Goths, whose father was Duke of Cordova. Nothing can be more melancholy than the neglected gardens, the broken fountains and statues, the empty fish-ponds, and grass-grown walks, despite the palms and orange-trees and luxuriant creeping roses, which seemed to be striving to conceal the desolation around. The first palm ever planted in Cordova was by the Moorish king Abdurrahman, who brought it from his much-loved and always regretted Damascus.

After luncheon, having obtained special permission from the archbishop, our party started off in two carriages for the hermitages in the Sierra Morena, stopping first at a picturesque ruined villa, called the 'Arrizafa,' once the favourite residence of the Moorish king. The gardens are beautiful; passion-flowers and jessamine hung in festoons over all the broken walls, and the ground was carpeted with violets, narcissus, and other spring flowers. The view from the terrace is lovely, the town, when seen from a distance, being very like Verona. Here the road became so steep that the party had to leave their carriages and walk the remainder of the way. The mountain-path reminded them of Mount Carmel, with the same underwood of cistus, lilac and white, and heaps of flowering and aromatic shrubs. Beautiful wild iris grew among the rocks, and half way up a rushing stream tumbled over the boulder-stones into a picturesque basin, covered with maiden-hair fern, which served as a resting-place for the tired travellers. After a fatiguing climb of two hours, they reached the postern gate of the hermitage, into which, after some demur as to their sex, the ladies, by special permission of the archbishop, were admitted. There are at present seventeen hermits, all gentlemen, and many of high birth and large fortune, living each in a little separate cabin, with a patch of garden round it, and entirely alone. They never see one another but at mass and in choir, or speak but once a month. In their chapel they have a beautiful oil painting of St. Paul, the first hermit, whose rule they follow in all its primitive severity. One of the cabins was vacant, and the party entered. It was composed of two tiny rooms : in the inner one was a bed formed of three boards, with a sheepskin and a pillow of straw ; the rest of the furniture consisted of a crucifix, a jug of water, a terrible discipline with iron points, and Rodriguez' essay on 'Christian Perfection,' published in 1606, at Valladolid, and evidently much read. This cell was that of Count ——, a man of great wealth and high rank, and of a still wider reputation for ability and talent. He had lost his wife some years ago, to whom he was passionately attached ; and remaining in the world only till he had settled his children, then took leave of it for ever, and resolved to spend the rest of his days in penitence and prayer. Their habit is composed of a coarse grey stuff, with a leathern girdle, drawers, and a shirt of serge. No linen is allowed, or stockings, and they wear sandals on their feet. They are not permitted to possess anything, or to keep anything in their cells but a glazed earthenware pot, a wooden plate, a pitcher, a lamp, and instruments of penance and devotion. They keep a perpetual fast on beans and lentils, only on high days and holidays being allowed fish. They are not allowed to write or receive letters, or to go into one another's cells, or to go out of the enclosure, except once a month, when they may walk in the mountains round, which they generally do together, reciting litanies. Seven hours of each day must be given to prayer, and they take the discipline twice a week.*   How strange a

---

* The Rev. Père Félix, the famous Paris preacher, in one of his Notre Dame conferences, speaking of asceticism of this sort, says : ' Les païens avaient épuisé la volupté : les chrétiens ont épuisé les souffrances. De ce creuset de la douleur l'homme nouveau a sorti, et c'est un homme plus grand que l'homme ancien. Ah ! je le sais, la pénitence corporelle, le jeûne, l'abstinence, la discipline, la flagellation, prêtent à rire à des penseurs de ce temps, qui se croient trop sages pour pratiquer de telles folies. Ils ont plus d'égard pour la chair, plus de respect surtout pour le corps, et ils disent en souriant à l'austérité chrétienne : " Ascétisme! Moyen âge! Fanatisme ! Démence !" La vérité est, que châtier volontairement son corps pour venger la dignité de l'homme outragée par les révoltes, est une

life for one accustomed to live in the world and
in society ! Yet there is no lack of candidates
for each vacancy; and the prior told our travellers that the number of vocations of late years
had increased. There is a fine old marble seat
and cross in the garden, erected by the late bishop,
from whence there is a magnificent view over the
whole country. The cold in winter is intense,
and they are not allowed any fires, except what
is absolutely necessary for the cooking of their
miserable meal. Taking leave of the prior in his
little ' parloir,' and receiving a rosary from him
made of the wood of the ' Carouba,' by the hermits themselves, the visitors retraced their steps
down the hill, feeling as if they had been spending
the last couple of hours in another world ; and,
rejoining their carriages at the villa, made the
circuit of the city walls, which are partly Moorish,
built of tapia, and described by Julius Cæsar.
Then one of the party went to see the Carmelite

sainte et sublime chose. La vérité est que pour accorder à son
corps le plaisir, il suffit d'être lâche, et que pour infliger à son corps
la douleur volontaire dans un but de restauration morale, il faut
être courageux, il faut être vraiment grand. La vérité est enfin que
cette race de mortifiés, mieux que tout autre, maintient à sa vraie
hauteur le niveau de l'humanité, et tient dans sa main intrépide,
avec le fouet dont elle se frappe elle-même, le drapeau du progrès.
Le chemin du progrès, comme celui du Calvaire, est un chemin dou-
loureux. Le drapeau de l'austérité chrétienne triomphera une fois
de plus dans le monde du sensualisme païen de nos jours.'

Convent of St. Theresa; not one of the saint's own foundation, but one built soon after her death. It contains twenty-four nuns, the cheeriest and merriest of women, proving how little external circumstances contribute to personal cheerfulness.

The German gentleman who had so kindly served as escort to our travellers during their stay at Cordova dined with them in the evening, and gave them several very interesting details of the place and people. · The next morning mass had been promised them at five, but it was six before the priest made his appearance in the fine old Jesuit church, now bereft of its pastors and frequent services; and it was only thanks to the unpunctuality of the Spanish railways, that the train which was to convey our party to Malaga was reached in time.

Passing through a very fine gorge of the Sierra Nevada, with magnificent Alpine scenery, the train suddenly stopped: the guard came to the carriages, and civilly suggested to the passengers that the government could not answer for the safety of the tunnels, and, therefore, had provided carriages and mules to take them round; or else, if they preferred it, that they might *walk*, as there would be plenty of time. This sounded ludicrous enough to

English ears, but, after all, they thought it more
prudent to comply than to run any risk, and accordingly bundled out with their bags and manifold packages.   On the recurrence of a similar
warning, however, a little later, they voted that
they would remain and take their chance; and
nothing disastrous occurred.   At the station they
were met by the kind and obliging English
consul, who had ordered rooms for them at the
hotel called the 'Alameda,' pleasantly situated on
the promenade, and who had done everything in
his power to ensure their comfort.   The first days
of their arrival were spent in settling themselves
in their new quarters, which required a good deal
of preliminary cleaning, and in seeing the so-
called 'lions' of the place.   These are soon visited.
In truth, except for climate, Malaga is as dull
and uninteresting a place as can be well imagined.   There is a cathedral, originally a mosque,
but now converted into an ugly Corinthian pile
with two towers.   Only one fine old Gothic door
remains, with curious 'azulejos.'   The rest, both
inside and out, is modern, heavy, and in bad taste.
The high altar, however, is by Alonso Caño; and
there is some fine wood-carving of the sixteenth
century in the choir and on the screen, com-
memorating different scenes in the life of St.

Malaga.

Turibius, Archbishop of Lima, whose apostolic labours among the Indians were crowned with such wonderful success. There are one or two good pictures and monuments, especially the recumbent figure of a bishop, in bronze, of the fifteenth century. In the sacristy is a valuable relic of St. Sebastian, and some fine silver vases for the holy oils; but everything else was plundered by the French. Afterwards our travellers went, with an order from the governor, to see the castle and Moorish fortress overlooking the town, built in 1279. Passing under a fine Moorish horse-shoe arched gateway, they scrambled up to the keep, from whence there is a magnificent view over sea and land. It is now used as a military prison, and about twenty-six men were confined there. The officers were extremely civil, and showed them everything. The men's barracks seemed clean and comfortable, and their rations good; their arms and knapsacks were, however, of the most old-fashioned kind. That day a detachment of troops were starting for Morocco, whose embarkation in the steamers below was eagerly watched by the garrison.

But if Malaga be dull in the way of sights, it is very pleasant from the kind and sociable character of its inhabitants. Nowhere will the stranger

E

find more genuine kindness, hospitality, or courtesy. Their houses, their villas, their horses, their flowers, their time, all are placed, not figuratively, but really, ' á vuestra disposicion.' Some of the villas in the neighbourhood are lovely, especially those of Madame de H——, the Marquise L—— &c. Here one finds all kinds of tropical vegetation : the date-palm, the banana, the plantain and Indian-rubber trees, sugar, cotton, and other Oriental products, all grow luxuriantly ; while the beds are filled with masses of violets, tulips, roses, arums, scarlet hybiscus, and geraniums ; and beautiful jessamine, *scarlet* passion-flowers, and other creepers, trail over every wall.

But the chief interest to the winter resident at Malaga will be derived from its charitable institutions. The French sisters of charity of St. Vincent de Paul have the care of three large establishments here. One—an industrial school for the children and orphans connected with a neighbouring factory—is a marvel of beauty, order, and good management. The girls are taught every kind of industrial work ; a Belgian has been imported to give them instruction in making Valenciennes lace, and their needlework is the most beautiful to be seen out of Paris. Any profit arising from their work is sold, and kept for their 'dot' when they marry or leave the establishment. Attached to this school is also a little home for widows, incurables, and sick, equally tended by the sisters. This admirable institution is the off-spring of individual charity and of a life wrecked—according to human parlance,—but which has taken heart again for the sake of the widow and the orphan, the sorrowful and the suffering. Her name is a household word in Malaga to the sad and the miserable; and in order to carry out her magnificent charities (for she has also an industrial school for boys in the country), she has given up her luxurious home, and lives in a small lodging up three pair of stairs. She reminded one of St. Jerome's description of St. Melania, who, having lost her husband and two children in one day, casting herself at the foot of the cross, exclaimed: 'I see, my God! that Thou requirest of me my whole heart and love, which was too much fixed on my husband and children. With joy I resign all to Thee.' The sight of her won-derful cheerfulness and courage, after sorrows so unparalleled, must strengthen every one to follow in her steps, and strive to learn, in self-abnega-tion, her secret of true happiness. The French sisters have likewise the charge of the great hos-pital of St. Juan de Dios, containing between

400 and 500 patients, now about to be removed to a new and more commodious building ; and also of a large day and infant school near the river, with a 'salle d'asile,' containing upwards of 500 children, who are daily fed with soup and bread. They also visit the poor and sick in their homes, and everywhere their steps are hailed with thankfulness and joy.

The 'Little Sisters of the Poor' have likewise established themselves in Malaga, and have a large house, containing seventy old and incurable people, which is very well supplied by the richer inhabitants. The nuns of the ' Assumption' have lately started a ' pension ' for the daughters of the upper classes, which was immensely wanted (education being at a very low ebb in Spain), and which has been most joyfully hailed by the Malaga ladies for their children. The superior, a charming person, is an Englishwoman ; and the frequent benediction services in their beautiful little chapel were a great boon to some of our party. They paid a visit also to the archbishop, a kind and venerable old man, with the most benevolent smile and aspect, and who is really looked upon as the father of his people. At a grand Te Deum service, given in the Church of S. Pietro dei Martiri, one of the most interesting churches in Malaga, as a thanksgiving for the preservation of the city from cholera, he officiated pontifically, which his great age generally prevents, and gave the benediction with mitre and crozier to the devout and kneeling multitude.

There is a very touching 'Via Crucis' service performed every Friday in Malaga, up to a chapel on the top of a high mountain overlooking the whole town and bay. The peasants chaunt the most plaintive and beautiful hymns, the words of which they 'improviser' on the way, both up and down. It begins at a very beautiful church and convent called Notre Dame des Victoires, now converted into a military hospital, nursed by the Spanish sisters of charity. The family of the Alcazars is buried in the crypt of this church, and beautiful palms grow in the convent garden. In the old refectory are some fine azulejos tiles and some good specimens of Raphael ware.

As to diversions, Malaga offers but few resources. Those who like boating may go out daily along the beautiful coast; but the rides are few, the ground hard and dusty, and the 'rivière à sec,' like that at Nice, must be traversed before any mountain expeditions could be reached. There is a bull-ring, as in every Spanish town, and occasionally the additional excitement of elephants being used in the fights : but the bulls will rarely face them.

After about a month, therefore, spent in this quiet little place, it was decided to start for Granada, which promised to afford greater interest and variety.

CHAPTER IV.

GRANADA.

TAKING leave rather sorrowfully of their many kind friends and of the sisters of charity who had been their constant companions during their stay in Malaga, our travellers started one stormy evening, and found themselves once more cooped up in one of those terrible diligences, and slowly ascending the mountains at the back of the town. Their intention had been to go on horseback, riding by Velez-Malaga and the baths of Alhama; but the late heavy rains had converted the mountain streams into torrents, and some of the party who attempted it were compelled to return. After ascending for about three hours, leaving on their left the picturesque cemetery, with its fine cypresses, they came to a plateau 3,000 feet above the sea, from whence they had a magnificent view, the whole of Malaga and its bay being stretched out at their feet, the lights glistening in the town, and the moon, breaking through the clouds, shedding a soft light

over the sea-line, which was covered with tiny fish-
ing-vessels. Beautiful aloes and cacti starting out
of the bold rocks on either side formed the foreground, while a rapid river rushed and tumbled in
the gorge below. But with this fine panoramic
view the enjoyment of our travellers came to an
end. When night came on, and they had reached
the highest and loneliest part of the bleak sierra,
it began to pour with rain and blow a regular
gale ; the heavy mud was dashed into their faces ;
the icy cold wind whistled through the broken
panes and under the floor of the carriage, and froze
them to the bone. There was some difficulty about
a relay of mules at the next stage, and so our
party were left on an exposed part of the road
without drivers or beasts for more than an hour.
Altogether, it was impossible to conceive a more
disagreeable journey ; and it was therefore with intense joy that they found themselves, after sixteen
hours of imprisonment, at last released, and once
more able to stretch their legs in the _Alameda_ of
Granada. Tired, hungry, dirty, and cold, a fresh
disappointment here awaited them. All the hotels were full (their letters ordering rooms had
miscarried), and only one tiny bedroom could be
found in which they could take refuge, and scrape
the mud off their clothes and hair. One of the

party found her way to the cathedral; the rest
held a council of war, and finally determined to
try their fate at the new 'Alhambra' hotel outside
the town, where an apartment was to be had, the
cold and wet of the season having deterred the
usual visitors to this purely summer residence.
They had every reason to congratulate themselves
on this decision; for though the cold was certainly
great, the snow hanging still on all the hills around,
and the house being unprovided with any kind of
fire-places or stoves, still the cleanliness and comfort of the whole amply compensated for these
drawbacks, to say nothing of the immense advantage of being close to the Alhambra, that great
object of attraction to every traveller who visits
Granada. The way up to it is very picturesque,
but very steep. After leaving the wretched, narrow, ill-paved streets, which dislocate almost every
bone in your body when attempted on wheels, and
passing by the Sala de la Audiencia and other fine
public buildings, you arrive at an arched gateway,
which at once brings you into a kind of public
garden, planted with fine English elms, and
abounding in walks and fountains and seats, and
in which the paths and drives, in spite of their precipitous character, are carefully and beautifully
kept by convict labour, under the superintendence

of a body of park-keepers dressed in full Andalusian costume.   The hotel is placed on the very
crest of the hill overlooking the magnificent range
of snowy mountains to the right.   To the left, the
first thing which strikes the eye is the Torre de
Justicia.   Over the outer horse-shoe arch is carved
an open hand, upon the meaning of which the
learned are divided; some saying it is an emblem
of the power of God, others a talisman against
the Evil Eye.   Over the inner arch is sculptured a
key, which typified the power of the Prophet over
the gates of heaven and hell.   A double gate pro-
tects this entrance, which no donkey may pass: in
the recess is a very beautiful little picture, framed
and glazed, of the Virgin and Child.   Passing
through this arch, you come to an open 'plaza,' out
of which rise two towers; one has been bought by
an Englishman, who has converted the lower part of
it into his private residence.   (Where shall we not
find our ubiquitous countrymen ?) *   The other is

---

* This unexpected rencontre reminded one of our party of a
similar surprise, some years ago, in the mountains of the Tyrol. She
was riding with her husband, when they came on a very picturesque
old 'schloss,' in an out-of-the-way gorge of a mountain pass.
Stopping to look at it, and pushing open a half-open door in what
appeared to be the only habitable part of the ruin, they came on a
group of chubby-faced English children, sitting round a table in
their white pinafores, eating an undeniable English tea; and were
told by the nurse, in answer to their enquiries, that the present

called the Torre de la Vela, because on this watch-
tower hangs the bell which gives warning to the
irrigators in the vega below. The view from hence
is the most enchanting thing possible, command-
ing the whole country. Below lies Granada with
its towers and sparkling rivers, the Darro and the
Xenil. Beyond stretches the beautiful rich 'vega'
(or plain), studded with villas and villages, and
encircled by snowy mountains, with the Sierra of
Alhama on one side, and the Gorge of Loja on
the other. Descending the tower, and standing
again in the 'plaza' below, you see opposite to
you a large ruined Doric palace, a monument of
the bad taste of Charles V., who pulled down a
large portion of the Moorish building to erect this
hideous edifice, which, like most other things in
Spain, remains unfinished. Passing through a
low door to the right, our travellers were perfectly
dazzled at the beauty which suddenly burst upon
them. It is impossible to conceive anything more
exquisite than the Alhambra, of which no drawings, no Crystal Palace models, not even Washington Irving's poetical descriptions, give one the
faintest idea. 'J'essaie en vain de penser : je ne

owner of this Austrian schloss was a London tradesman, who brought
his children over every year to spend the summer—a most sensible
arrangement, as the healthy bright looks of his little ones testified.

peux que sentir !' exclaimed the authoress of 'Les Lettres d'Espagne' on entering ; but the predominant feeling is one of regret for the Moors, whose dynasty produced such marvels of beauty and of art. Entering by the fish-pond ' patio,' and visiting first the Whispering Gallery, you pass through the Hall of the Ambassadors, and the Court of Lions, out of which lead the Hall of the Abencerrages, and that of Justice, with its two curious monuments and wonderful fretted roof, and then come to the gem of the whole, the private apartments of the Moorish kings, with the recessed bedroom of the king and queen, the boudoir and lovely latticed windows overlooking the beautiful little garden of Lindaraja (the violets and orangeblossoms of which scented the whole air), and the exquisite baths below.* It is a thing to dream of,

---

* Few have described this enchanting palace as well as the French lady already quoted. She says, speaking of the feelings it calls forth :—' J'aimerais autant être broyée dans la gueule de ces jolis monstres qui ont des nez en nœud de cravate, appelés *Lions* par la grâce de Mahomet, que de te parler de l'Alhambra, tant cette description est difficile. Les murailles ne sont que guipures délicates et compliquées : les plus hardies stalactites ne peuvent donner une idée des coupoles. Le tout est une merveille, un travail d'abeilles ou de fées. Les sculptures sont d'une délicatesse ravissante, d'un goût parfait, d'une richesse qui vous fait songer à tout ce que les contes de fées vous décrivaient jadis à l'heureux âge où l'imagination a des ailes d'or. Hélas ! la mienne n'a plus d'aile, elle est de plomb. Les Arabes n'employaient que quatre couleurs : le bleu, le rouge, le noir

and exceeds every previous expectation. Again
and again did our travellers return, and always
discovered some fresh beauties. The governor resides in a modernised corner of the building, not
far from the mosque, which has suffered from the
bad taste of the Christian spoilers. He is not a
good specimen of Spanish courtesy, as, in spite of
letters of introduction from the highest quarters,
it was with very great difficulty that our party
were admitted to see anything beyond the portions of the building open to the general public.
At last, however, he condescended to find the keys
of the Tower of the Infantas, once the residence
of the Moorish princesses whose tragical fate is so
touchingly recorded by Washington Irving. It
is a beautiful little cage, overlooking the ravine,
with its fine aqueduct below, and rich in the
delicate moresque carving of both ceilings and
walls. Afterwards, crossing a garden, they came to
the gate by which Boabdil left his palace for the
last time, and which was afterwards, by his special
request, walled up. The tower at this corner
was mined and destroyed by the French. Our
party then descended to a little mosque lately

et l'or. Cette richesse, ces teintes vives, sont visibles encore partout.
Enfin, mon ami, ce n'est point un palais ceci : c'est la ville d'un
enchanteur !'

purchased by Colonel ——, and beautifully restored. This completed the circuit of the Alhambra, which is girdled with walls and towers
of that rich red-brown hue which stands out so
beautifully against the deep blue sky, but the
greater portion of which was ruthlessly destroyed
by Sebastiani, at the time of his occupation of
Granada.

The restoration of this matchless palace has
been undertaken by the present queen, who has
put it in the hands of a first-rate artist named
Contreras ; and this confidence has been well be-
stowed, for it is impossible to see work executed in
a more perfect manner, so that it is very difficult
to tell the old portions from the new. If he be
spared to complete it, future generations will see
the Alhambra restored very nearly to its pristine
beauty. This gentleman makes exquisite models
of different parts of the building, done to a scale,
which are the most perfect miniature fac-similes
possible of the different portions of this beautiful
palace, and a most agreeable memento of a visit
to it. Our travellers purchased several, and only
regretted they had not chosen some of the same
size, as they would make charming panels for a
cabinet or screen.

In the afternoon, the party started to see the

cathedral, escorted by the kind and good-natured dean, who engaged the venerable mother of the 'Little Sisters of the Poor' to act as his interpreter, his Andalusian Spanish being utterly unintelligible to most of the party. The first feeling on entering is of unmixed disappointment. It is a Pagan Greco-Roman building, very much what our London churches are which were erected in the time of the Georges. But it has one redeeming point—the Capilla de los Reyes, containing the wonderful monuments of Ferdinand and Isabella, and of Philip and Joan. The alabaster sepulchres of the former, wrought at Genoa by Peralta, are magnificent, both in design and execution. Isabella's statue is especially beautiful :

> . . . . . . In questa forma
> Passa la bella donna, e par che dorma.

The faces are both portraits, and have a simple dignity which arrests the attention of the most unobservant. A low door and a few steep steps below the monuments lead to their last resting-place. The royal coffins are of lead, lapped over, rude and plain (only the letter F distinguishes that of the king), but they are genuine, and untouched since the day when their bodies, so justly revered by the Spaniards, were deposited in this humble vault.

Among the treasures of this chapel are likewise shown the identical royal standards used at the conquest of Granada; the king's sword; the queen's own missal; their crozier and crown of silver-gilt; the picture of the Virgin and Child by St. Luke, given to Isabella by Pope Innocent VIII., and before which mass is said every 2nd of January, the anniversary of the taking of the city; and the portrait of the knight who, during the siege, rode into Granada, and affixed a taper and an 'Ave Maria' on the very door of the principal mosque. In the sacristy is a 'Conception,' exquisitely carved, by Alonso Caño; an 'Adoration of the Kings,' by Hemling, of Bruges; a curious ring of Sixtus II.; a chasuble embroidered by Queen Isabella; some very valuable relics and reliquaries, and a letter of St. Charles Borromeo, which the good-natured dean allowed one of the party to copy. Besides these treasures, and the Capilla de los Reyes, there is really nothing to look at in the cathedral, but one or two good painted glass windows, some clustered columns, and a curious arch in the dome, which was made to bend downwards.

The following morning, after an early service at the Capuchin convent of St. Antonio, one of the party started on an expedition with the sisters of the town, and winding up a beautiful and steep ravine, in the holes and caverns of which gipsies live and congregate, they came to a picturesque wood planted on the side of the mountain. Here they left their carriages, and scrambled up a zig-zag path cut in the hill, with low steps or 'gradini,' till they reached a plateau, on which stands both convent and church. The view from the terrace in front is the most magnificent which can be conceived. On one side are the snowy mountains of the Sierra Nevada, with a rapid river tumbling into the gorge below, the valleys being lined on both sides with stone-pine woods, amid which little convents and villages are clustered. On the other is the town of Granada, with its domes and towers; and sharply standing out on the rocks above the ruins, against the bright blue sky, are the coffee-coloured towers of the beautiful Alhambra. There is a Via Crucis up to this spot, the very crosses seeming to start up out of the rocks, which are clothed with aloes and prickly pear; while in the centre of the terrace is a beautiful fountain and cross, shaded by magnificent cypresses. The church is built over some catacombs, where the bodies of St. Cecilia and of eleven other martyrs were found, who suffered in the persecution under Nero. The superior of this

F

convent, now converted into a college, is Don José Martin, a very holy man, though quite young, and revered by the whole country as a saint. He is a wonderful preacher, and by his austere and penitential life works miracles in bringing souls to God. His manner is singularly gentle, simple, and humble. He kindly came to escort the party through the catacombs, and to show them the relics. The sites of the different martyrdoms have been converted into small chapels or oratories : in one, where the victim perished by fire, his ashes still remain. Little leaden tablets mark the different spots. Here also is the great wooden cross of St. John of the Cross, from the foot of which he preached a sermon on the 'Love of God' during his visit to Granada, which is said to have converted upwards of 3,000 people. 'I always come here to pray for a few minutes before preaching,' said simply Don José Martin, 'so that a portion of his spirit may rest upon me.' After spending some time in this sanctuary, the party reluctantly retraced their steps, and returned to the town, where they had promised to visit the great hospital of San Juan de Dios. It is a magnificent establishment, entirely under the care of the Spanish sisters of charity of St. Vincent de Paul, with a 'patio' or quadrangle in the centre, and double cloisters round, into which the wards open : all round the cloisters are frescoes describing different scenes in the life of the saint. The church is gorgeous in its decorations, and in a chapel above rests the body of San Juan, in a magnificent silver shrine, with his clothes, his hat, the basket in which he used daily to go and collect food for his sick and dying poor, and other like personalties.

This saint is immensely revered in Granada. He was the first founder of the Order of Brothers of Charity, now spread all over Europe, beginning his great work, as all the saints have done, in the humblest manner possible, by hiring a small house (now converted into a wayside oratory), in which he could place four or five poor people, nursing them himself night and day, and only going out to beg, sell, and chop wood, or do anything to obtain the necessary food and medicines for them. The archbishop, touched with his burning charity, assisted him to build a larger hospital. This house soon after took fire, when San Juan carried out the sick one by one on his back, without receiving any hurt. It is thus that he is represented in the Statue Gallery of Madrid. The people, inflamed by his loving zeal, and in admiration of his great wisdom, humility, and

prudence, came forward as one man to help him
to build the present hospital, which remains to this
day as a monument of what may be done by one
poor man of humble birth, if really moved by the
love of God. His death was caused by rescuing
a man in danger of drowning from the sudden
rising of the river, and then remaining, wet and
worn out as he was, while caring for the family.
He died on his knees, repeating the 'Miserere,'
amidst the tears of the whole city, to whom, by
the special command of the archbishop, he gave
his dying benediction. His favourite saying was :
'Labour without intermission to do all the good
works in your power while time is allowed you ;'
and this sentence is engraved in Spanish on the
door of the hospital.

The following day happened to be the anniversary of his death, or rather of his birthday in
heaven, when a touching and beautiful ceremonial
is observed. The archbishop and his clergy come
to the hospital to give the Holy Communion to
the sick in each ward. A procession is formed
of the ecclesiastics and the sisters of charity, each
bearing lighted tapers, and little altars are
arranged at the end of each ward, beautifully
decorated with real flowers, while everything in
and about the hospital is fresh and clean for the

occasion. A touching incident occurred in the
male ward on that day, where one poor man lay
in the last stage of disease. The eagerness of his
look when the archbishop drew near his bed will
never be forgotten by those who were kneeling
there; nor the way in which his face lighted up
with joy when he received His Lord. The atten-
dant sister bent forward to give him a cordial
afterwards : he shook his head, and turned his face
away; he would have nothing after *That.* Before
the last notes of the ' Pange Lingua ' or the curling
smoke of the incense had died out of the ward,
all was over; but the smile on the lips and the
peace on the face spoke of the rest he had found.
Afterwards there was a magnificent service in
the church, and a dinner to all the orphans in the
sisters' schools.

Another interesting expedition made by our
travellers was to the Carthusian convent outside
the town. Sebastiani desecrated and pillaged the
wonderful treasures it contained ; but the tortoise-
shell and mother-of-pearl doors and presses remain, reminding one of those in the Armenian
Church at Jerusalem at the shrine of St. James.
There are also two statues of St. Bruno, by Alonso
Caño ; wonderful for their life-like appearance
and expression, but still not equal to the incom-

parable one at Miraflores. There are some beautiful alabaster and agate pillars still left in the
chapel behind the high altar, which it is to be supposed were too heavy for the spoilers to carry off.
In the cloisters are some curious frescoes of the
martyrdoms of the Carthusians, at the time of the
Protestant Reformation, by Henry VIII. of England. The guide who accompanied our travellers
said slyly to the only Catholic of the party : 'We
had better not explain the subject of these. Let
them imagine they are some of the horrors of
the Inquisition,—*that always takes with English
people!*' Another picture was startling both in
subject and colouring; it was that of a dead doctor. much venerated in life, who, on a funeral pane-
gyric being pronounced over him, started from his
coffin, exclaiming 'that his life had been a lie,
and that he was among the damned!' The friar
who showed our party over the now deserted convent was like Fray Gabriel in Fernan Caballero's
novel of 'La Gaviota.' When the rest of the
Carthusians were turned out by the government,
he would not go. 'I was brought here as a little
child,' he said, 'and know no one in the world;'
and so he sat himself down by the cross and
sobbed. They let him stay and keep the garden
and the church, but his life is over. 'The blood

does not run in his veins—it walks!' Like Fray
Gabriel, he will die kneeling before the Christ to
whom he daily prays for those who have so cruelly
wronged and robbed him. The view from the terrace in front of the church is beautiful, overlooking
the rich and cultivated plain of Soto de Roma,
the property of the Duke of Wellington, with
the mountain of Parapanda above, the hills of
Elvira, and the pass of Moclin, which forms the
bridle-road to Cordova. The gardens also are
delightful : no wonder the poor monks clung to
their convent home !

In the afternoon our travellers walked up to
the Generalife, a villa now belonging to the
Pallavicini family, a branch of the great Genoa
house, but formerly the palace of the Sultana.
Passing through vineyards and fig-trees, they
arrived at the gate of the fairy garden, with its
long straight borders, fringed with myrtle, irri-
gated by the Darro, which is carried in a little
canal between the flower-beds, and with a beautiful open colonnade overlooking the Alhambra,
while a less formal garden sent up a shower
of sweet scents from the orange-trees and jessamine trellises below. Through this colonnade
they passed into the living-rooms, exquisite in
their Moorish carvings and decorations. In one of

them there are a number of curious though somewhat apocryphal portraits, including one of Boabdil, and of another Moorish king of Granada, with
his wife and daughter, who turned Christians, and
were baptized at Santa Fé.   In the outer room
are portraits of all the 'bluest blood' of Granada.
But the gardens form the greatest charm.   The
ground was covered with Neapolitan violets and
other spring flowers.   Roses climbed over every
wall, and magnificent cypresses, and aloes in full
flower, shaded the beds from the burning sun.
The largest of these cypresses, called the Sultana,
is twelve feet in circumference, and to this tree
the fatal legend of the fair Zoraya is attached.
Behind these cypresses is a flight of Italian-looking
steps, leading to another raised garden, full of
terraces and fountains.   On the steep brow of the
hill is an alcove, or summer-house, from whence
the views over Granada and the Alhambra are
quite enchanting, every arch being, as it were, the
setting or frame of a new and beautiful picture.
Above this again is a Moorish fortress, and a
knoll called the Moor's Chair, from whence the
last Moorish king is said to have sadly contemplated the defeat of his troops by the better dis-
ciplined armies of Ferdinand and Isabella grouped
in the plains below.   Scrambling still higher up,

our travellers came to the ruins of a chapel, and to
some curious caverns, with a peep into a wild gorge
to the right, leading into the very heart of this
mountainous and little visited region. Boabdil's
sword, and other relics and pictures of the fifteenth
century belonging to the Pallavicini family, are
carefully preserved by their agent in their house in
the town, and had been courteously shown to our
travellers when they called to obtain permission to
visit the villa. Returning towards their hotel, they
thought they would prolong their walk by visiting
the great cemetery, or ' Campo Santo,' which is a
little to the north of the Generalife. Long files
of mourners had been perpetually passing by their
windows, the bier being carried on men's shoulders,
and uncovered, as in the East, so that the face
of the dead was visible. Each bier was followed
by the confraternity to which he or she belonged,
chanting hymns and litanies as they wound up
the long steep hill from the town to the burial-
ground. But all appearance of reverence, or even
of decency, disappears at the spot itself, where
the corpse is stripped, taken out of its temporary
coffin, and brutally cast into a pit, which is kept
open till filled, and then, with quicklime thrown
in, closed up, and a fresh one opened to be treated
in a similar manner. It is a disgrace to Catholic

Spain that such scenes should be of daily recurrence.

Another villa worth visiting in the neighbourhood of the Alhambra is that of Madame Calderon, where the obliging French gardener took our
travellers all over the gardens and terraces, the
hot-houses and aviaries, the artificial streams and
bridges, till they came to the great attraction of
the place—a magnificent arbor vitæ, or hanging
cypress, falsely called a cedar of Lebanon, which
was planted by St. John of the Cross, this site
being originally occupied by a convent of St.
Theresa's. The house is thoroughly comfortable
inside, with charming views over the ' vega,' and
altogether more like an English home than anything else in Spain. If anyone wished to spend
a delightful summer out of England, they could
find no more agreeable retreat; perfect as to
climate, and with the most enjoyable and beautiful expeditions to be made in every direction.
It is worth remembering, as Madame Calderon,
being now a widow, is anxious to let her residence, having another house in Madrid. There is
a church close by, and a dairy attached to the
garden, which is a rarity in Spain, and a public
benefit to the visitors at the Alhambra; and the
clever and notable French wife of the gardener

makes delicious butter, and sells both that and
the cream in her mistress's absence—luxuries
utterly unknown anywhere else in the Peninsula.

Bad weather and heavy snow (for they had
visited Granada too early in the year) prevented
our travellers from accomplishing different expeditions which they had planned for the ascent of the Sierra Nevada, and visiting Alhama
and Adea and other interesting spots in the
neighbourhood. But they drove one day to the
Alameda, where all Granada congregates in the
evening, and from whence the view looking on
the mountains is beautiful.

Returning by the Moorish gateway, called the
Puerta de Monayma, they came to an open
space, in the centre of which is a statue of the
Virgin. Here public executions used to take place,
and here, in 1831, Mariana Pineda, a lady of high
birth and great beauty, was strangled. A simple
cross marks the spot. Her crime was the finding
in her house a flag, maliciously placed there by
a man whose addresses she had rejected.

From this 'plaza' our travellers drove to the
conflux of the rivers Darro and Xenil, which
together form the Guadalquiver; and from thence
proceeded to a mosque, where a tablet records
the fact of its having been the place where the

unfortunate king Boabdil gave the keys of the town to the Christian conquerors, Ferdinand and Isabella, and then himself rode slowly and sadly away from his beautiful palace by a mountain still called the 'Last Sigh of the Moor,' immortalised both in verse and song. The accompanying ballad, with its plaintive wailing sound, still echoes in the hearts and on the lips of the people.

Ay de mi Alhama!

Pasoabaso el Rey Mo—ro Por la ciudad de Granada, Desde la puerta de Elvira Hasta la de Bibarrambla.

Ay de mi Alhama!

Returning, they visited the Church of Las Angustias, where there is a wonderful but tawdrily dressed image of the Blessed Virgin, who is the patroness of the town. The French sisters of charity have a large orphanage and day-school here, established originally by Madame Calderon ; but the situation, in the street called Recogidas, is low and damp, and their chapel being almost underground, and into which no sun can ever enter, seriously affects the health of the sisters. Here, as everywhere, they are universally beloved and respected, and the present superior is one eminently qualified, by her loving gentleness and evenness of temper, to win the hearts of all around her. The dress of the people in Granada is singularly picturesque : the women wear crape shawls of the brightest colours, yellow, orange, or red, with flowers stuck jauntily on one side of the head just above the ear ; the men have short velvet jackets, waistcoats with beautiful hanging silver buttons (which have descended from father to son, and are not to be bought except by chance), hats with large borders, turned up at the edge, red sashes round the waist, and gaiters of untanned leather, daintily embroidered, open at the knee, with hanging strips of leather and silver buttons. Over the whole, in cold weather, is thrown the ' capa,' or large cloak, which often conceals the threadbare garments of a beggar, but which is worn with the air of the proudest Spanish ' hidalgo.' This evening, the last which our travellers were to spend in Granada, they had a visit from the king and captain of the gipsies, a very remarkable man, between thirty and forty years of age, and a blacksmith by trade. He brought his guitar, and played in the most marvellous and beautiful way possible : first tenderly and softly; then bursting into the wildest exultation; then again plaintive and wailing, ending with a strain of triumph and rejoicing and victory which completely entranced his hearers. It was like a beautiful poem or a love-tale, told with a pathos indescribable. It was a fitting last remembrance of a place so full of poetry and of the past, with a tinge in it of that sorrowful dark thread which always seems woven into the tissue of earthly lives. Sorrowfully, the next morning, our travellers paid their last visit to the matchless Alhambra, which had grown upon them at every turn. Then came the 'good-bye' to their good and faithful guide, *Bensaken*, that name so well known to all Granada tourists; and to the kind sisters of charity, whose white 'cornettes' stood grouped round the fatal diligence which was to convey them back to Malaga. And so they bade adieu to this beautiful city, with many a hope of a return on some future day, and with a whole train of new thoughts and new pictures in their mind's eye, called forth by the wonders they had seen.

CHAPTER V.

THE journey from Granada was, if possible, more wearying than before, for the constant heavy rains had reduced the roads to a perfect Slough of Despond, in which the wretched mules perpetually sank and fell, and were flogged up again in a way which, to a nature fond of animals, is the most insupportable of physical miseries. Is there a greater suffering than that of witnessing cruelty and wrong which you are powerless to redress? It was not till nearly eleven o'clock the following day that our travellers found themselves once more in their old quarters on the Alameda of Malaga. By the kindness of the superior of the hospital, the usual nine o'clock mass had been postponed till the arrival of the diligence: and very joyfully did one of the party afterwards take her old place at the refectory of the community, whose loving welcome made her forget that she was still in a strange land. The following three or four days were spent almost entirely in making preparations for their journey to Gibraltar, viâ Ronda, that eagle's nest, perched on two separate rocks, divided by a rapid torrent, but united by a picturesque bridge, which crowns the range of mountains forming the limits of the kingdom of Granada. The accounts of the mountain-path were not encouraging ; but to those who had ridden for four months through the Holy Land, no track, however rugged and precipitous, offered any terrors. But when the time came, to their intense disappointment, the road was found to be impassable on the Gibraltar side, owing to the tremendous torrents, which the heavy rains had swollen to a most unusual extent. Two officers had attempted to swim their horses over ; but in so doing one of them was drowned, so that there seemed no alternative but to give up their pleasant riding expedition, and, with it, the sight of that gem of the whole country which had been one of their main objects in returning to Malaga. Comforting themselves, however, by the hope of going there later from Seville, our travellers took berths in the steamer 'Cadiz,' bound for Gibraltar ; and after a beautiful parting benediction at the little convent of the Nuns of the Assumption, they took leave of their many kind friends, and, at six o'clock (accompanied by

Madame de Q—— and her brother to the water's edge), stepped on board the boat which was to convey them to their steamer. Their captain, however, proved faithless as to time; and it was not till morning that the cargo was all on board and the vessel under weigh for their destination. After a tedious and rough passage of nineteen hours, they rounded at last the Europa Point, and found themselves a few minutes later landing on the Water Port Quay of the famous rock. Of all places in Spain, Gibraltar is the least interesting, except from the British and national point of view. Its houses, its people, its streets, its language, all are of a detestably mongrel character.*

* The able authoress from whom we have already quoted expresses herself on Gibraltar as follows :—

'Gibraltar est bâti à l'Anglaise : les "cottages" sont laids et incommodes sous ce ciel brûlant. Pour voitures, des paniers d'osier. Les Anglaises ont six pieds, les Anglais sept et demi. Ils mettent de grands fichus de mousseline blanche sur leurs chapeaux, quoiqu'il ne fasse pas encore chaud ; ils font de grands pas avec de grands pieds. Ah ! ce n'est plus l'Andalousie, ce n'est plus la mantille ! Les chapeaux des dames viennent de la rue St.-Denis. Plus de grâce, plus de charme, plus de poésie, plus de repos ; mais un terrible remue-ménage. . . . Je suis logée au Club-House Hotel, dans une espèce de salle de spectacle, à colonnes corinthiennes, qui donne sur la place. La place est laide, les arbres sont rabougris. Je vois passer les Maures, portant avec noblesse leurs vêtements blancs aux longs plis, d'autres ont des robes éclatantes, quelques-uns ont les jambes nues. Nous avons été par delà le Mont des Singes. Je n'en ai pas vu un—personne n'en a jamais vu !'—*Lettres d'Espagne*, pp. 180-181.

G

The weather, too, during our travellers' stay, was essentially British, incessant pouring rain and fog alternating with gales so tremendous that twenty vessels went ashore in one day. Nothing was to be seen from the windows of the Club-House Hotel but mist and spray, or heard but the boom of the distress gun from the wrecking ships, answered by the more cheering cannon of the port. But there is a bright side to every picture : and one of the bright sides of Gibraltar is to be found in its kind and hospitable governor and his wife, who, nobly laying aside all indulgence in the life-long sorrow which family events have caused, devote themselves morning, noon, and night to the welfare and enjoyment of everyone around them. Their hospitality is natural to their duties and position ; but the kind consideration which ever anticipates the wishes of their guests, whether residents or, as our travellers were, birds of passage, here to-day and gone to-morrow, springs from a rarer and a purer source.

Another object of interest to some of our party was the charitable institutions of the place. The white 'cornettes' of the sisters of charity are not seen as yet ; but the sisters of the ' Bon Secours ' have supplied their place in nursing the sick and tending all the serious cases of every class

in the garrison. Their value only became fully
known at the late fearful outbreak of cholera, to
which two of them fell victims : but they seemed
rather encouraged than deterred by this fact.
They live in a house half-way up the hill on the
way to Europa Point, which contains a certain
number of old and incurable people and a few
orphan children. They visit also the sick poor
in their homes, and in the Civil Hospital, which
is divided, drolly enough, not into surgical and
medical wards, but according to the *religion* of
the patients ! one half being Catholic, the other
Protestant, and small wards being reserved likewise
for Jews and Moors. It is admirably managed, the
patients are supplied with every necessary, and
well cared for by the kind-hearted superinten-
dent, Dr. G——. The ' Dames de Lorette' have
a convent towards the Europa Point, where they
board and educate between twenty and thirty
young ladies. They have also a large day-school
in the town for both rich and poor, the latter
being below and the former above. The children
seem well taught, and the poorer ones were remarkable for great neatness and cleanliness. The
excellent and charming Catholic bishop, Dr.
Scandella, Vicar Apostolic of Gibraltar, has built
a college for boys on the ground adjoining his

palace, above the convent, from whence the view is glorious : the gardens are very extensive. This college, which was immensely needed in Gibraltar, is rapidly filling with students, and is about to be affiliated to the London University. In the garden above, a chapel is being built to receive the Virgin of ' Europa,' whose image, broken and despoiled by the English in 1704, was carried over to Algeciras, and there concealed in the hermitage ; but has now been given back by Don Eugenio Romero to the bishop, to be placed in this new and beautiful little sanctuary overlooking the Straits, where it will soon be once more exposed to the veneration of the faithful. The bishop has lately built another little church below the convent, dedicated to St. Joseph, but which, from some defect in the materials, has been a very expensive undertaking.

It was very pleasant to see the simple, hearty, manly devotion of the large body of Catholic soldiers in the garrison, among whom his influence has had the happiest effect in checking every kind of dissatisfaction and drunkenness. His personal influence has doubtless been greatly enhanced by his conduct during the cholera, when he devoted himself, with his clergy, to the sick and dying, taking regular turns with them in the administration of the Last Sacraments, and only claiming as his privilege that of being the one always called up in the night, so that the others might get some rest. He has two little rooms adjoining the church, where he remains during the day, and receives anyone who needs his fatherly care.

The Protestant bishop of Gibraltar, a very kind and benevolent man, resides at Malta, and has a cathedral near the governor's house, lately beautified by convict labour, and said to be well attended. It is the only Protestant church in Spain.

Of the sights of Gibraltar it is needless to speak. Our travellers, in spite of the weather, which rarely condescended to smile upon them, visited almost everything : the North Fort, Spanish Lines, and Catalan Bay, one day ; Europa Point, with the cool summer residence of the governor (sadly in need of government repair), and St. Michael's Cave, on the next ; and last, not least, the galleries and heights. From the Signal Tower the view is unrivalled ; and the aloes, prickly pear, and geranium, springing out of every cleft in the rock, up which the road is beautifully and skilfully engineered, add to the enjoyment of the ride. The gentlemen of the party hunted in the cork woods when the weather would allow of it ;

and the only 'lion' unseen by them were the monkeys, who resolutely kept in their caves or on the African side of the water during their stay at Gibraltar. The garden of the governor's palace is very enjoyable, and contains one of those wonderful dragon-trees of which the bark is said to bleed when an incision is made. The white arums grow like a weed in this country, and form most beautiful bouquets when mixed with scarlet geranium and edged by their large bright shining green leaves.

The time of our travellers was, however, limited, especially as they wished to spend the Holy Week in Seville. So, after a ten days' stay, reluctantly giving up the kind offer of the Port Admiral to take them across to Africa, and contenting themselves with buying a few Tetuan pots from the Moors at Gibraltar, they took their passages on board the 'London' steamer for Cadiz.

By permission of the governor, they were allowed to pass through the gates after gun-fire, and got to the mole; but there, from some mistake, no boat could be found to take them off to their vessel, and they had the pleasure of seeing it steam away out of the harbour without them, although their passages had been paid for, and, as they thought, secured. In despair, shut out of

the town, where a state of siege, for fear of a
surprise, is always rigorously maintained by the
English garrison, they at last bribed a little boat
to take them to a Spanish vessel, the ' Allegri,'
likewise bound for Cadiz, and which was advertised to start an hour later. In getting on board
of her, however, they found she was a wretched tub,
heavily laden with paraffine, among other combus-
tibles, and with no accommodation whatever for
passengers. There was, however, no alternative
but going in her or remaining all night tossing
about the harbour in their cockle-shell of a boat ;
so they made up their minds to the least of the
two evils, and a few minutes later saw them
steaming rapidly out of the harbour towards
Cadiz. The younger portion of the party found
a cabin in which they could lie down : the elder
lay on the cordage of the deck, and prayed for a
cessation of the recent fearful storms, the captain
having quietly informed them that in the event
of its coming on to blow again he must throw all
their luggage overboard as well as a good deal of
his cargo, as he was already too heavily laden to
be safe. However, the night was calm, though
very cold, and the following morning saw them
safely rounding the forts of Cadiz, and staring at
its long low shores. But then a new alarm seized

them. The quarantine officers came on board
with a horrible yellow flag, and talked big about
the cholera having reappeared at Alexandria, and
the consequent impossibility of their being able to
produce a clean bill of health. The prospect of
spending a week in that miserable vessel, or in the
still more dismal lazaretto on the shore, was anything but agreeable to our travellers. However,
on the assurance of the captain that the only
vessel arrived from Egypt before they left Gibraltar had been instantly put into quarantine by
the governor, they were at last allowed to land
in peace, and found very comfortable rooms at
Blanco's Hotel, on the promenade, their windows
and balconies looking on the sea.

In the absence of the bishop, who was gone to
Tetuan, Canon L—— kindly offered his services
to show them the curiosities of the town, and took
them first to the Capuchin convent, now converted
into a madhouse, in the church adjoining which are
two very fine Murillos : one, ' St. Francis receiving the Stigmata,' which, for spirituality of expression, is really unrivalled ; the other, ' The Marriage
of St. Catherine,' which was his *last* work, and is
unfinished. The great painter fell from the scaf-
folding in 1682, and died very soon after, at
Seville, in consequence of the internal injuries he

PEARSON JC.

had received. From this convent they proceeded
to the cathedral, which is ugly enough, but where
the organ and singing were admirable. The
stalls in the choir, which are beautifully carved,
were stolen from the Cartucha at Seville. There
is a spacious crypt under the high altar, with a
curious flat roof, unsupported by any arches or
columns, but at present it is bare and empty.
Their guide then took them to see the workhouse,
or 'Albergo dei Poveri,' an enormous building,
which is even more admirably managed than the
one at Madrid. It contains upwards of a thousand
inmates. The boys are all taught different trades,
and the girls every kind of industrial and needle
work. The dormitories and washing arrangements are excellent ; and all the walls being lined,
up to a certain height, with the invariable blue
and white ' azulejos,' or glazed tiles, gives a clean,
bright appearance to the whole. The dress of
the children was also striking to English eyes,
accustomed to the hideous workhouse livery at
home. On Sundays they have a pretty and varied
costume for both boys and girls, and their little
tastes are considered in every way. They have a
large and handsome church, and also a chapel for
the children's daily prayers, which they themselves
keep nice and pretty, and ornament with flowers

from their gardens. The whole thing is like a
' *home* ' for these poor little orphans, and in painful contrast to the views which Protestant England takes of charity in her workhouses, where
poverty seems invariably treated as a crime. The
children are in a separate wing of the building—the girls above, the boys below. On the
other side are the sick wards, and those for the
old and incurable, where the same minute care
for their comfort and pleasure is observed in every
arrangement. Nor is there that horrible prison
atmosphere, and that locking of doors as one
passes through each ward, which jars so painfully
on one's heart in going through an English workhouse. There are very few able-bodied paupers ;
and those are employed in the work of the house
and garden. There is a spacious ' patio,' or court,
with an open colonnade of marble columns, running round the quadrangle, the centre of which is
filled with orange-trees and flowers. This beautiful
palace was founded and endowed by the private
benevolence of one man, who dedicated it to St.
Helena, in memory of his mother, and placed in
it the sisters of charity of St. Vincent de Paul,
who have the entire care of the whole establishment. There are fifteen sisters, all Spaniards,
but affiliated to the French ones, and with the

portrait of N. T. H. Père Étienne in the place of honour in their 'parloir' and refectory. The superior is a most remarkable woman, little and 'contrefaite,' but with a soul in her eyes which it is impossible to forget. The institution is now in the hands of the government, who have wisely not attempted to make any alterations in the administration. There are upwards of fifty of these sisters of charity in Cadiz, they having the sole charge of the hospitals, schools, workhouses, &c. ; and the admirable cleanliness, order, and comfort in each which is the result, must commend them to the intelligent approval of every visitor, even should he be unmoved by the evidence of that unpaid charity which, with its soft finger-touch, stamps all their works with the very essence of Divine love.

The next day being Palm Sunday, our travellers went to service in the cathedral. It was very fine, but extremely fatiguing. There are no chairs or seats in Spanish churches. Everyone kneels on the floor the whole time, not even rising for the Gospel or Creed. On one of the party attempting to stand up at the long Gospel of the Passion, she was somewhat indignantly pulled down again by her neighbours. During the sermon, the Spanish women have a peculiar way of sitting on their heels—a process which they learn from childhood, but which to strangers is an almost intolerable penance. Here, as everywhere in Spain, the hideous fashion of bonnets or hats was unknown, and the universal black mantilla, with its graceful folds and modest covering of the face, and the absence of all colours to distract attention in the house of God, made our English ladies sigh more eagerly than ever for a similar reverent and decent fashion to be adopted at home. On returning for the vesper service in the afternoon, a beautiful, and, to them, novel, custom was observed. At the singing of the 'Vexilla Regis,' the canons, in long black robes, knelt prostrate in a semicircle before the high altar, and were covered by a black flag with a red cross. This they saw repeated daily during the Passion Week services at Seville. In the evening there was a magnificent Benediction and Processional service round the cloisters of the church called 'Delle Scalze.' It was impossible to imagine anything more picturesque than the multitude kneeling in the open 'patio,' or court, shaded by orange-trees, and full of beautiful flowers, while round the arches swept the gorgeous procession carrying the Host, the choir and people singing alternate verses of the

' Lauda Sion,' the curling smoke of the incense
reflecting prismatic colours in the bright sunshine,
and the whole procession finally disappearing in
the sombre dark old church, of which the centre
doors had been thrown wide open to receive it.
One longed only for Roberts's paint-brush to
depict the scene. Returning to their hotel, our
party found the Alameda gay with holiday folk,
and full of the ladies whose beauty and charm have
been the pride of Cadiz for so many generations.
Do not let our readers think it invidious if we
venture on the opinion that their beautiful and
becoming dress has a great deal to do with this,
just as, in the East, every turbaned Turk or
burnoused Arab would make a perfect picture.
Dress your Oriental in one of Poole's best fitting
coats and trousers, and give him a chimney-pot
hat, and where would be his beauty ? In the same
way, if—which good taste forefend—the Spanish
ladies come to imagine that a bonnet stuck on
the back of the head, and every colour in the
rainbow, is prettier than the flowing black robe
and softly folded lace mantilla, shading modestly
their bright dark eyes and hair, they will find, to
their cost, that their charm has vanished for ever.

Nothing more remained to be seen or done in
Cadiz but to purchase some of the beautiful mats

which are its great industry, and which are made
of a flat reed or 'junco,' growing in the neighbourhood ; and these the kind and good-natured
English consul undertook to forward to them,
when ready, to England.

Giralda, Seville.

CHAPTER VI.

SEVILLE.

ARMED with sundry letters of introduction sent them from Madrid, our travellers started by early train for Seville, the amiable Canon L—— having given them a five o'clock mass before starting, in his interesting old circular church dedicated to S. Filippo Neri, he being one of the Oratorians. They passed by Xeres, famous for its sherry cellars, called 'bodegas,' supplying more wine to England than to all the rest of the world put together, and for its Carthusian convent, once remarkable for its Zurbaranpictures, the greater portion of which have now followed the sherry to the British Isles; then by Alcalà, noted for its delicious bread, with which it supplies the whole of Seville, for its Moorish castle and beautiful river Aira, the waters of which, after flowing round the walls of the little town, are carried by an aqueduct to Seville; and so on and on, through orange and olive groves, and wheat plains, and

vineyards, till the train brought them by mid-day
to the wonderful and beautiful city which had
been the main object of their Spanish tour.

The saying is strictly true :

> Quien no ha visto Sevilla,
> No ha visto maravilla.

Scarcely had they set foot in their comfortable
hotel, the 'Fonda de Londres,' when an obliging
aide-de-camp of the Spanish general came to tell
them that if they wanted to see the Alcazar they
must go with him at once, as the infanta, who
had married the sister of the king's consort,
was expected with his wife to occupy the palace
that evening, when it would naturally be closed
to visitors. Dusty, dirty, and hot as they were,
therefore, they at once sallied forth with their
kind cicerone and the English consul for this
fairy palace of the Moors. Entering by the Plaza
del Triunfo, under an arched gateway, where
hangs, day and night, a lamp throwing its soft
light on the beautiful little picture of the Virgin and Child, they came into a long court, in
the midst of which are orange-trees and fountains,
and this again led them by a side door into the
inner court or 'patio' of the palace.

Like the Alhambra, it is an exquisite succession of delicate columns, with beautifully carved

Alcazar, Seville.

capitals, walls, and balconies, which look as if
worked in Mechlin lace; charmingly cool 'patios,'
with marble floors and fountains; doors whose
geometrical patterns defy the patience of the
painter; horse-shoe arches, with edges fringed like
guipure; fretted ceilings, the arabesques of which
are painted in the most harmonious colours, and
tipped with gold; lattices every one of which
seems to tell of a romance of beauty and of love:
such are these moresque creations, unrivalled in
modern art, and before which our most beautiful
nineteenth century palaces sink into coarse and
commonplace buildings. They are the realisation of the descriptions in the 'Arabian Nights,'
and the exquisite delicacy of the work is not its
sole charm. The *proportions* of every room, of
every staircase, of every door and window, are perfect: nothing offends the eye by being too short or
too wide. In point of sound also, they, as well as
the Romans, knew the secret which our modern
builders have lost; and in harmony of colour, no
'azulejos' of the present day can approach the
beauty and brilliancy of the Moorish tints. Nor
are historical romances wanting to enhance the
interest of this wonderful place. In the bed-
chamber of the king, Pedro the Cruel, are painted
three dead heads, and thereon hangs a tale of

II

savage justice. The king overheard three of his
judges combining to give a false judgment in a
certain case about which they had been bribed, and
then quarrel about their respective shares of their
ill-gotten spoils. He suddenly appeared before
them, and causing them to be instantly beheaded,
placed their heads in the niches where now the
paintings perpetuate the remembrance of the
punishment. Less excusable was another tragedy
enacted within these walls, in the assassination of
the brother of the king, who had been invited as a
guest, and came unsuspicious of treachery. A deep
red stain of blood in the marble floor still marks
the spot of the murder. Well may Spain's most
popular modern poet, the Duque de Rivas, in his
beautiful poem, exclaim :—

> Aun en las losas se mira
> Una tenaz mancha oscura ; . . .
> Ni las edades la limpian ! . . .
> Sangre ! sangre ! Oh cielos ! cuantos,
> Sin saber que lo es, la pisan ! *

The gardens adjoining the palace are quaintly
beautiful, the borders edged with myrtle and box,
cut low and thick, with terraces and fountains,
and kiosks, and 'surprises' of 'jets d'eau,' and
arched walls festooned with beautiful hanging

* 'One still sees on the pavement a dark spot—the lapse of ages
has not effaced it ! Blood ! blood ! O Heaven ! how many tread
it under foot without knowing it !'

creepers, and a ' luxe ' of Oriental vegetation. On
one side are the white marble baths, cool and
sombre, where the beautiful Maria de Padilla
forgot the heat and glare of the Seville sun. It
was the custom of the courtiers in her day to
drink the water in which the ladies had bathed.
Pedro the Cruel reproached one of his knights
for not complying with this custom. 'Sire,' he
replied, 'I should fear lest, having tasted the
sauce, I should covet the bird!'

The Alcazar formerly extended far beyond its
present limits; but the ruined towers by the
water-side are all that now remain to mark the
course of the old walls.

Our travellers could not resist one walk through
the matchless cathedral on their way home; but
reserved their real visit to that and to the Giralda
till the following day. The kind Regente de la
Audiencia and his wife, to whom they had
brought letters of introduction, came to them in
the evening, and arranged various expeditions for
the ensuing week.

Early the next morning the Countess L——
de R—— came to fetch one of the party to
the Church of S. Felipe Neri, which, like all the
churches of the Oratorians, is beautifully decorated,
and most devout and reverent in its services. It

is no easy matter to go on wheels in the streets
of Seville. There are but two or three streets in
which a carriage can go at all, or attempt to turn ;
and so to arrive at any given place, it is generally
necessary to make the circuit of half the town.
In addition to this, the so-called pavement, an-
gular, pointed, and broken, shakes every bone in
one's body. To reach their destination on this
particular morning, our friends had to traverse
the market-place, and make an immense détour
through various squares, passing meanwhile by
several very interesting churches ; but it was all
so much gain to the stranger.

After mass, one of the fathers, who spoke
English, kindly showed them the treasures of his
church, and among other things a beautiful silver-
chased chapel behind the high altar, containing
some exquisite bénitières, crucifixes, and relics.
The wooden crucifixes of Spain, mostly carved by
great men, such as Alonso Caño or Montanés,
are quite wonderful in beauty and force of expression ; but they are very difficult to obtain.
They have a pretty custom in this church of
offering two turtle doves in a pure white basket
when a child is devoted to the Blessed Virgin,
which are left on the altar, as in the old days of the
Purification, and the white basket is afterwards

laid up in the chapel. After breakfast the whole
party arrived at the cathedral. How describe
this wonderful building! To say it is such and
such a height, and such and such a width, that it
has so many columns, and so many chapels, and
so many doors, and so many windows. . . . Why,
Murray has done that far better than anyone
else! But to understand the cathedral at Seville,
you must know it; you must feel it; you must
live in it; you must see it at the moment of the
setting sun, when the light streams in golden
showers through those wonderful painted glass
windows (those chefs-d'œuvre of Arnold of Flanders), jewelling the curling smoke of the incense still hanging round the choir; or else go
there in the dim twilight, when the aisles seem to
lengthen out into infinite space, and the only
bright spot is from the ever-burning silver lamps
which hang before the tabernacle.

One of the party, certainly not given to admiration of either churches or Catholicity, exclaimed
on leaving it : 'It is a place where I could not
help saying my prayers!' The good-natured
Canon P—— showed them all the treasures and
pictures. They are too numerous to describe in
detail; but some leave an indelible impression.
Among these is Murillo's wonderful 'St. Antony,'

in the baptistery ; Alonso Caño's delicious little
'Virgin and Child' (called 'Nuestra Señora de
Belem') ; Morales' 'Dead Christ ;' a very curious
old Byzantine picture of the Virgin ; and in the
sacristy, the exquisite portraits by Murillo of
St. Leander, Archbishop of Seville, the great
reformer of the Spanish liturgy, whose bones
rest in a silver coffin in the Capilla Real, and
of St. Isidore, his brother, who succeeded him in
the see, called the 'Excellent Doctor,' and whose
body rests at Leon.   Here also is a wonderful
'Descent from the Cross,' by Campana, before
which Murillo used to sit, and say 'he waited till
He was taken down ;' and here, by his own particular wish, the great painter is buried.   There
is besides a fine portrait of S. Teresa ; and
round the handsome chapter-room are a whole
series of beautiful oval portraits by Murillo, and
also one of his best 'Conceptions.'   Among the
treasures is the cross made from the gold which
Christopher Columbus brought home from America, and presented to the king ; the keys of
the town given up to Ferdinand by the Moorish
king at the conquest of Seville ; two beautiful
ostensorios of the fifteenth century, covered with
precious stones and magnificent pearls ; beautiful
Cinquecento reliquaries presented by different

Popes; finely illuminated missals in admirable preservation; an exquisitely carved ivory crucifix; wonderful vestments, heavy with embroidery and seed-pearls; the crown of King Ferdinand; and last, not least, a magnificent tabernacle altar-front, angels and candlesticks, all in solid silver, beautiful in workmanship and design, used for Corpus Christi, and other solemn feasts of the Blessed Sacrament. One asks oneself very often: ' How came all these treasures to escape the rapacity of the French spoilers ? '

The Royal Chapel contains the body of St. Ferdinand, the pious conqueror of Seville, which town, as well as Cordova, he rescued from the hands of the Moors, after it had been in their possession 524 years. This pious king, son to Alphonse, King of Leon, bore witness by his conduct to the truth of his words on going into battle: ' Thou, O Lord, who searchest the hearts of men, knowest that I desire but Thy glory, and not mine.' To his saint-like mother, Berangera, he owed all the good and holy impressions of his life. He helped to build the Cathedral of Toledo, of which he laid the first stone, and, in the midst of the splendours of the court, led a most ascetic and penitential life. Seville surrendered to him in 1249, after a siege of sixteen months, on which

occasion the Moorish general exclaimed, that
'only a saint, who, by his justice and piety, had
won Heaven over to his interest, could have taken
so strong a city with so small an army.' By the
archbishop's permission, the body of the saint was
exposed for our travellers. It is in a magnificent silver shrine ; and the features still retain a
remarkable resemblance to his portraits. His
banner, crown, and sword were likewise shown to
them, and the little ivory Virgin which he always
fastened to the front of his saddle when going to
battle. The cedar coffin still remains in which
his body rested previous to its removal to this
more gorgeous shrine. On the three days in the
year when his body is exposed, the troops all
attend the mass, and lower their arms and colours
to the great Christian conqueror. A little staircase at the back of the tomb brings you down
into a tiny crypt, where, arranged on shelves, are
the coffins of the beautiful Maria Padilla, of Pedro
the Cruel, and of their two sons : latterly, those of
the children of the Duc and Duchesse de Montpensier have been added. Over the altar of the
chapel above hangs a very curious wooden statue
of the Virgin, given to St. Ferdinand by the good
king Louis of France. King Ferdinand adorned
her with a crown of emeralds and a stomacher of

diamonds, belonging to his mother, on condition that they should never be removed from the image.

The organs are among the wonders of this cathedral, with their thousands of pipes, placed horizontally, in a fan-like shape. The ' retablo ' at the back of the high altar is a marvel of wood-carving ; and the hundreds of lamps which burn before the different shrines are all of pure and massive silver. One is tempted to ask : ' Was it by men and women like ourselves that cathedrals such as this were planned and built and fur-nished ? ' The chapter who undertook it are said to have deprived themselves even of the necessa-ries of life to erect a basilica worthy of the name ; and in this spirit of voluntary poverty and self-abnegation was it begun and completed. Never was there a moment when money was so plen-tiful in England as now, yet where will a cathe-dral be found built since the fifteenth century ?

At the west end lies Fernando, son of the great Christopher Columbus, who himself died at Val-ladolid, and is said to rest in the Havana. The motto on the tomb is simple but touching :—

Á Castilla y á Leon, mundo nuevo dió Colon.

Over this stone, during Holy Week, is placed

the 'monumento,' an enormous tabernacle, more
than 100 feet high, which is erected to contain
the Sacred Host on Holy Thursday : when lighted
up, with the magnificent silver custodia, massive
silver candlesticks, and a profusion of flowers and
candles, it forms a 'sepulchre' unequalled in the
world for beauty and splendour.

Passing at last under the Moorish arch towards
the north-east end of the cathedral, our travellers
found themselves in a beautiful cloistered 'patio,'
full of orange-trees in full blossom, with a magnificent fountain in the centre. In one corner is
the old stone pulpit from which St. Vincent Ferrer,
St. John of Avila, and other saints preached to
the people : an inscription records the fact. Over
the beautiful door which leads into the cathedral
hang various curious emblems : a horn, a croco-
dile, a rod, and a bit, said to represent plenty,
prudence, justice, and temperance. To the left
is the staircase leading to the Columbine Library,
given by Fernando, and containing some very
interesting MSS. of Christopher Columbus. One
book is full of quotations, in his own handwriting,
from the Psalms and the Prophets, proving the
existence of the New World ; another is a plan
of the globe and of the zodiac drawn out by him.
There is also a universal history, with copious notes,

in the same bold, clear, fine handwriting; and a
series of his letters to the king, written in Latin.
Above the book-shelves are a succession of curious
portraits, including those of Christopher Columbus and his son Fernando, which were given by
Louis Philippe to the library; of Velasquez; of
Cardinal Mendoza; of S. Fernando, by Murillo;
and of our own Cardinal Wiseman, who, a native
of Seville, is held in the greatest love and veneration here. A touching little account of his life
and death has lately been published in Seville by
the talented Spanish author, Don Leon Carbonero
y Sol, with the appropriate heading 'Sicut vita
finis ita.' Our party were also shown the sword
of Fernand Gonsalves, a fine two-edged blade,
which did good service in rescuing Seville from
the Moors.

Redescending the stairs, our travellers mounted
the beautiful Moorish tower of the Giralda,
built in the twelfth century by Abu Yusuf Yacub,
who was also the constructor of the bridge of
boats across the Guadalquiver. This tower forms
the great feature in every view of Seville, and is
matchless both from its rich yellow and red-brown
colour, its sunken Moorish decorations, and the
extreme beauty of its proportions. It was originally 250 feet high, and built as a minaret,

from whence the Muezzin summoned the faithful to prayers in the mosque hard by ; but Ferdinand Riaz added another 100 feet, and, fortunately, in perfect harmony with the original design. He girdled it with a motto from Proverbs xviii. : 'Nomen Domini fortissima turris.'

The ascent is very easy, being by ramps sloping gently upwards. The Giralda is under the special patronage of SS. Justina and Rufina, daughters of a potter in the town, who suffered martyrdom in 304 for refusing to sell their vessels for the use of the heathen sacrifices. Sta. Justina expired on the rack, while Sta. Rufina was strangled. The figure which crowns the tower is that of Faith, and is in bronze, and beautifully carved.

The bells are very fine in tone ; but what repays one for the ascent is the view, not only over the whole town and neighbourhood, but over the whole body of the huge cathedral, with its forest of pinnacles and its wonderfully constructed roof, which looks massive enough to outlast the world. The delicate Gothic balustrades are the home of a multitude of hawks (the *Falco tinunculoides*), who career round and round the beautiful tower, and are looked upon almost as sacred birds.

The thing which strikes one most in the look

of the town from hence is the absence of streets.
From their excessive narrowness, they are invisible at this great height, and the houses seem all
massed together, without any means of egress or
ingress. The view of the setting sun from this
tower is a thing never to be forgotten ; nor the
effect of it lit up at night, when it seems to hang
like a brilliant chandelier from the dark blue
vault above.

Tired as our travellers were, they could not
resist one short visit that afternoon to the Museum, and to that wonderful little room below,
which contains few pictures only, but those few
unrivalled in the world.

Here, indeed, one sees what Murillo could do.
The ' St. Thomas of Villanueva,' giving alms to
the beggar (called by the painter himself his
own picture) ; the ' St. Francis ' embracing the
crucified Saviour ; the ' St. Antony,' with a lily in
adoration before the infant Jesus ; the ' Nativity ; '
the ' San Felix de Cantalicia,' holding the infant
Saviour in his arms which the Blessed Virgin is
coming down to receive ; the ' SS. Rufina and Justina ; ' and last, not least, the Virgin which earned
him the title of ' El Pintor de las Concepciones.'
Each and all are matchless in taste, in expression, in feeling ; above all, in devotion. It is

impossible to meditate on any one of these mysteries in our Blessed Lord's life without the recollection of one of these pictures rising up instantly
in one's mind, as the purest embodiment of the
love, or the adoration, or the compunction, which
such meditations are meant to call forth : they are
in themselves a prayer.

In the evening one of the party went with the
Regent to call on the venerable Cardinal Archbishop, whose fine palace is exactly opposite the
east front of the cathedral. It was very sad to
wind up that fine staircase, and see him in that
noble room, groping his way, holding on by the
wall, for he is quite blind. It is hoped, however,
that an operation for cataract, which is contemplated, may be successful. He was most kind, and
gave the English stranger a place in the choir of
the cathedral for the Processional services of the
Holy Week and Easter—a great favour, generally
only accorded to royalty, and of which the lady
did not fail to take advantage. M. Leon Carbonero y Sol, the author and clever editor of the
'Crux,' paid them a visit that evening. By his
energy and perseverance this monthly periodical
has been started at Seville, which is an event in
this non-literary country; and he has written
several works, both biographical and devotional,

which deserve a wider reputation than they have yet obtained.

The following day, being Wednesday in Holy Week, the whole party returned to the cathedral, to see the impressive and beautiful ceremony of the Rending of the White Veil, and the 'Rocks being rent,' at the moment when that passage is chanted in the Gospel of the Passion. The effect was very fine; and all the more, from the sonibre light of the cathedral, every window in which was shaded by black curtains, and every picture and image shrouded in black.* At vespers, the canons, as at Cadiz, knelt prostrate before the altar, and were covered with the black red-cross flag. At four o'clock our travellers went to the Audiencia, where the Regent and his kind wife had given them all seats to see the processions. How are these to be described? They are certainly appreciated by the people themselves; but they are not suited to English taste, especially in the glare of a Seville sun : and unless representations of the terrible and awful events connected with our Lord's Passion be depicted with the skill of a great artist, they become simply intensely painful. The thing which was touching and beautiful was

---

* Faber says very beautifully : 'Passion-tide veils the face of the crucifix, only that it may be more vivid in our hearts.'

the orderly arrangement of the processions themselves, and the way in which men of the highest
rank, of royal blood, and of the noblest orders, did
not hesitate to walk for hours through the dusty,
crowded, burning streets for three successive
days, with the sole motive of doing honour to
their Lord, whose badge they wore. To show
the importance attached by the good people
of Seville to this portion of the Holy Week
services, the programme is inserted verbatim in
the Appendix.

The processions invariably ended by passing through the cathedral and stopping for
some minutes in the open space between the
high altar and the choir. The effect of the
brilliant mass of light thrown by thousands of
wax tapers, as the great unwieldy catafalque
was borne through the profound darkness of the
long aisles, was beautiful in the extreme; and
representations which looked gaudy in the sunshine were mellowed and softened by the contrast
with the night. The best were 'The Sacred
Infancy,' the 'Bearing of the Cross,' and the
'Descent from the Cross.' In all, the figures were
the size of life, and these three were beautifully
and naturally designed. Less pleasing to English
eyes, in spite of their wonderful splendour, were

those of the Blessed Virgin, decked out in gorgeous velvet robes, embroidered in gold, and covered with jewels, with lace pocket-handkerchiefs in the hand, and all the paraphernalia of a fine lady of the nineteenth century! It is contrary to our purer taste, which thinks of her as represented in one of Raphael's chaste and modest pictures, with the simple robe and headdress of her land and people; or else in the glistening white marble, chosen by our late beloved Cardinal as the fittest material for a representation of her in his 'Ex Voto,' and which speaks of the spotless purity of her holy life. Leaving the house of the Regent, the party made their way with difficulty through the dense crowd to the cathedral, where the Tenebræ began, followed by the Miserere, beautifully and touchingly sung, without any organ accompaniments, at the high altar. It was as if the priests were pleading for their people's sins before the throne of God. The next day was spent altogether in these solemn Holy Thursday services. After early communion at the fine Church of S. Maria Magdalena, thronged, like all the rest, with devout worshippers, our party went to high mass at the cathedral, after which the Blessed Sacrament, according to custom, was carried to the gigantic 'monumento,' or sepulchre,

I

before mentioned, erected at the west door of the cathedral, and dazzling with light. Then came the 'Cena' in the archbishop's palace, at which his blindness prevented his officiating; and then our travellers went round the town to visit the 'sepulchres' in the different churches, one more beautiful than the other, and thronged with such kneeling crowds, that going from one to the other was a matter of no small difficulty. The heat also increased the fatigue; and here, as at Palermo, no carriages are allowed from Holy Thursday till Easter Day: everyone must perform these pious pilgrimages on foot. At half-past two, they went back to the cathedral for the Washing of the Feet. An eloquent sermon followed, and then began the Tenebræ and the Miserere as before, with the entry of the processions between: the whole lasted till half-past eleven at night.

Good Friday was as solemn as the same day is at Rome or at Jerusalem. The Adoration of the Cross in the cathedral was very fine: but women were not allowed to kiss it as in the Holy City. After that was over, some of the party, by the kind invitation of the Duc and Duchesse de Montpensier, went to their private chapel, at St. Elmo, for the 'Tre Ore d' Agonie,' being from

twelve to three o'clock, or the hours when our
Saviour hung upon the cross. It was a most
striking and impressive service. The beautiful
chapel was entirely hung with black, and pitch
dark. On entering, it was impossible to see one's
way among the kneeling figures on the floor, all,
of course, in deep mourning. The sole light was
very powerfully thrown on a most beautiful picture of the Crucifixion, in which the figures were
the size of life. The sermon, or rather meditation
on the seven words of our Lord on the cross, was
preached by the superior of the oratory of S.
Felipe Neri, a man of great eloquence and personal holiness. It would be impossible to exag-
gerate the beauty and pathos of two of these
meditations; the one on the charity of our
Blessed Lord, the other on His desolation. A
long low sob burst from the hearts of his hearers
at the conclusion of the latter. The wailing
minor music between was equally beautiful and
appropriate; it was as the lament of the angels
over the lost, in spite of the tremendous sacrifice!
At half-past three, the party returned to the
cathedral, where the services lasted till nine in
the evening, and then came home in the state of
mind and feeling so wonderfully represented by
De la Roche, in the last portion of his 'Good

Friday' picture. Beautifully does Faber exclaim :
' The hearts of the saints, like sea-shells, murmur
of the Passion evermore.'

The Holy Saturday functions began soon after
five the next morning, and were as admirably
conducted as all the rest. Immense praise was
due to the ' maestro de ceremonias,' who had
arranged services so varied and so complicated
with such perfect order and precision : and the
conduct of the black-veiled kneeling multitude
throughout was equally admirable ; one and all
seemed absorbed by the devotions of the time
and season.

That evening, the Vigil of Easter, was spent in
the cathedral by some of our party in much the
same manner as they had done on a preceding one
in the Holy City two years before. The night
was lovely. The moon was streaming through
the cloisters on the orange-trees of the beautiful
' patio,' across which the Giralda threw a deep
sharp shadow, the silver light catching the tips of
the arches, and shining with almost startling
brightness on the ' Pietà ' in the little wayside
chapel at the south entrance of the court. All
spoke of beauty, and of peace, and of rest, and of
stillness, and of the majesty of God. Inside the
church were groups of black or veiled figures,

Doorway of Cathedral at Seville.

mostly women (were not women the first at the sepulchre ?), kneeling before the tabernacle, or by the little lamps burning here and there in the side chapels. Each heart was pouring forth its secret burden of sorrow or of sin into the Sacred Heart which had been so lately pierced to receive it. At two in the morning matins began, ' Hæc dies quam fecit Dominus ;' and after matins a magnificent Te Deum, pealed forth by those gigantic organs, and sung by the whole strength of the choir and by the whole body of voices of the crowd, which by that time had filled every available kneeling space in the vast cathedral. Then came a procession ; all the choristers in red cassocks, with white cottas and little gold diadems. High mass followed, and then low masses at all the side altars, with hundreds of communicants, and the Russian salutation of ' Christ is risen !' on every tongue. It was ' a night to be remembered,' as indeed was all this Holy Week : and now people seemed too happy to speak ; joy says short words and few ones. Many have asked : ' Is it equal to Jerusalem or Rome ?' In point of services, 'Yes;' in point of interest, ' No :' for the presence of the Holy Father in the one place, and the vividness of recollection which the actual scenes of our Blessed Lord's Passion inspires in the other, must

ever make the Holy and Eternal Cities things
apart and sacred from all besides. But nowhere
else can 'fonctions' be seen in such perfection
or with such solemnity as at Seville. Everything
is reverently and well done, and nothing has
changed in the ceremonial for the last 300 years.

A domestic sorrow had closed the palace of the
Duc and Duchesse de Montpensier as far as their
receptions were concerned; but they kindly gave
our party permission to see both house and
gardens, which well deserve a visit. The palace itself reminded them a little of the Duc d'Aumale's
at Twickenham: not in point of architecture,
but in its beautiful and interesting contents; in
its choice collections of pictures, and books, and
works of art, and in the general tone which per-
vaded the whole. There are two exquisite Murillos; a 'St. Joseph' and a 'Holy Family;' a
Divino Morales; a 'Pietà;' some beautiful Zurbarans; and some very clever and characteristic
sketches by Goya. They have some curious historical portraits also, and some very pretty modern
pictures. The rooms and passages abound in
beautiful cabinets, rare china, sets of armour,
African trappings, and Oriental costumes. In
the snug low rooms looking on the garden, and
reminding one of Sion or of Chiswick, there are

little fountains in the centre of each, combining
Oriental luxury and freshness with European
comfort. The gardens are delicious. They contain a magnificent specimen of the 'palma regis,'
and quantities of rare and beautiful shrubs ; also
an aviary of curious and scarce birds. You
wander for ever through groves of orange, and
palms, and aloes, and under trellises covered with
luxuriant creepers and clustering roses, with a
feeling of something like envy at the climate,
which seems to produce everything with comparatively little trouble or culture. To be sure
there is 'le revers de la médaille,' when the
scorching July sun has burnt up all this lovely
vegetation. But the spring in the garden of St.
Elmo is a thing to dream about.

From this enjoyable palace our party went
on to visit 'Pilate's House,' so called because
built by Don Enrique de Ribera, of the exact
proportions of the original, in commemoration
of his pilgrimage to Jerusalem in 1519. It is
now the property of the Duque de Medina
Sidonia. Passing into a cool 'patio,' you see
a black cross, marking the first of the stations
of a very famous Via Crucis, which begins here
and ends at the Cruz del Campo outside the
town. There is a pretty little chapel opening out

of the 'patio,' ornamented with Alhambra work,
as is all the rest of this lovely little moresque
palace. It is a thorough bit of Damascus, with
its wonderful arabesqued ceilings, and lace-like
carvings on the walls and staircases, and cloistered 'patios,' and marble floors and fountains.
Behind is a little garden full of palms, orange-
trees, and roses in full flower, and, at the time
our travellers saw it, carpeted with Neapolitan
violets; quaint low hedges, as in the Alcazar
gardens, divided the beds, and broken sculpture
lay here and there.

One of the great treasures of Seville had
yet been unvisited by our party, and that was
the Lonja, formerly the Exchange, a noble
work of Herrera's. It stands between the cathedral and the Alcazar, and is built in the shape
of a great quadrangle, each side being about
200 feet wide. Ascending the fine marble staircase, they came to the long 'sala' containing
the famous 'Indian Archives,' that is, all the
letters and papers concerning the discovery of
South America. There are thousands of MS.
letters, beautifully arranged and docketed; and
among them the autographs of Fernando Cortes,
Pizarro, Magellan, Americo Vespuzio (who could
not write his own name, and signed with a mark),

Fra Bartolomeo de las Cazas, and many others.
There is also the original Bull of the Pope,
granting the new South American discoveries
to the Spaniards; and another, defining the
rights between the Spaniards and the Portuguese
in the matter of the conquered lands. The
librarian, a very intelligent and good-natured
personage, also showed them a curious list, sent
home and signed by Fernando Cortes, of the
silks, painted calabashes, feathers, and costumes
presented by him to the king; and a quantity of
autograph letters of Charles V., Ferdinand and
Isabella, and of Philip IV. Fernando Cortes died
at Castilleja, on December 3, 1547, and the following day his body was transported to the family
vault of the Duque de Medina Sidonia, in the
monastery of San Isidoro del Campo. The Due
de Montpensier has purchased the house, and
made a collection of everything belonging to the
great discoverer, including his books, his letters,
various objects of natural history, and some very
curious portraits, not only of Cortes himself, but
of Christopher Columbus, Pizarro, Magellan, the
Marques del Valle (of the Sicilian family of
Monteleone), Bernal Diaz, Velasquez, of the his-
torian of the conquest of Mexico, Don Antonio
Solis, and many others.

In the afternoon, the Marques de P—— called for our travellers to take them to the University, and to introduce them to the rector and to the librarian, whose name was the well-deserved one of Don José Bueno, a most clever and agreeable man, whose pure Castilian accent made his Spanish perfectly intelligible to his English visitors. He very good-naturedly undertook to show them all the most interesting MSS. himself, together with some beautiful missals, rare first editions of various classical works, and some very clever etchings of Goya's of bull fights and ladies—the latter of doubtful propriety. In the church belonging to the University are some fine pictures by Roelas and Alonso Caño, some beautiful carvings by Montañés, and several very fine monuments. In the rector's own room is a magnificent 'St. Jerome,' by Lucas Kranach, the finest work of that artist that exists. There are 1,200 students in this University, which rivals that of Salamanca in importance.

Taking leave of the kind librarian, the Marques de P—— went on to show them a private collection of pictures belonging to the Marques Cessera. Amidst a quantity of rubbish were a magnificent 'Crucifixion,' by Alonso Caño ; a Crucifix, painted on wood, by Murillo, for an infirmary, and con-

cealed by a Franciscan during the French occupation in 1812 ; a Zurbaran, with his own
signature in the corner ; and, above all, a 'Christ
bound with the Crown of Thorns,' by Murillo,
which is the gem of the whole collection, and
perfectly beautiful both in colouring and expression.

Coming home, they went to see. the house to
which Murillo was taken after his accident at
Cadiz, and where he finally died ; also the site of
his original burial, before his body was removed
to the cathedral where it now rests.

But one of the principal charms of our travellers' residence in Seville has not yet been
mentioned ; and that was their acquaintance,
through the kind Bishop of Antinoe, with Fernan Caballero. She may be called the Lady
Georgiana Fullerton of Spain, in the sense of
refinement of taste and catholicity of feeling.
But her works are less what are commonly called
novels than pictures of home life in Spain, like
Hans Andersen's ' Improvisatore,' or Tourgeneff's
' Scènes de la Vie en Russie.'

This charming lady, by birth a German on the
father's side, and by marriage connected with all
the ' bluest blood ' in Spain, lives in apartments
given her by the queen in the palace of the

Alcazar. Great trials and sorrows have not dimmed the fire of her genius or extinguished one spark of the loving charity which extends itself to all that suffer. Her tenderness towards animals, unfortunately a rare virtue in Spain, is one of her marked characteristics. She has lately been striving to establish a society in Seville for the prevention of cruelty to animals, after the model of the London one, and often told one of our party that she never left her home without praying that she might not see or hear any ill-usage to God's creatures. She is no longer young, but still preserves traces of a beauty which in former years made her the admiration of the court. Her playfulness and wit, always tempered by a kind thoughtfulness for the feelings of others, and her agreeableness in conversation, seem only to have increased with lengthened experience of people and things. Nothing was pleasanter than to sit in the corner of her little drawing-room, or, still better, in her tiny study, and hear her pour out anecdote after anecdote of Spanish life and Spanish peculiarities, especially among the poor. But if one wished to excite her, one had but to touch on questions regarding her faith and the so-called 'progress' of her country. Then all her Andalusian blood

would be roused, and she would declaim for
hours in no measured terms against the spolia-
tion of the monasteries, those centres of education
and civilisation in the villages and outlying
districts; against the introduction of schools
without religion, and colleges without faith; and
the propagation of infidel opinions through the
current literature of the day.

Previous acquaintance with the people had already made some of our travellers aware of the
justice of many of her remarks. Catholicism in
Spain is not merely the religion of the people;
it is their life. It is so mixed up with their
common expressions and daily habits, that, at
first, there seems to a stranger almost an irreverence in their ways. It is not till you get
thoroughly at home, both with them and their
language, that you begin to perceive that holy
familiarity, if one may so speak, with our Divine
Lord and His Mother which impregnates their
lives and colours all their actions. Theirs is a
world of traditions, which familiarity from the
cradle have turned into faith, and for that faith
they are ready to die. Ask a Spanish peasant
why she plants rosemary in her garden? She
will directly tell you that it was on a rosemary-
bush that the Blessed Virgin hung our Saviour's

clothes out to dry as a baby. Why will a
Spaniard never shoot a swallow? Because it
was a swallow that tried to pluck the thorns out
of the crown of Christ as He hung on the cross.
Why does the owl no longer sing? Because he
was by when our Saviour expired, and since then
his only cry is 'Crux! crux!' Why are dogs
so often called Melampo in Spain? Because it
was the name of the dog of the shepherds who
worshipped at the manger at Bethlehem. What
is the origin of the red rose? A drop of the
Saviour's blood fell on the white roses growing
at the foot of the cross—and so on, for ever!
Call it folly, superstition—what you will. You
will never eradicate it from the heart of the
people, for it is as their flesh and blood, and
their whole habits of thought, manners and customs, run in the same groove. They have, like
the Italians, a wonderful talent for 'improvis-
ing' both stories and songs; but the same beautiful thread of tender piety runs through the
whole.

One day, Fernan Caballero told them, an old
beggar was sitting on the steps of the Alcazar:
two or three children, tired of play, came and sat
by him, and asked him, child-like, for 'a story.'
He answered as follows :—'There was once a

hermit, who lived in a cave near the sea. He was a very good and charitable man, and he heard that in a village on the mountain above there was a very bad fever, and that no one would go and nurse the people for fear of infection. So up he toiled, day after day, to tend the sick, and look after their wants. At last he began to get tired, and to think it would be far better if he were to move his hermitage up the hill, and save himself the daily toil. As he walked up one day, turning this idea over in his mind, he heard some one behind him saying: "One, two, three." He looked round, and saw no one. He walked on, and again heard : "Four, five, six, seven." Turning short round this time, he beheld one in white and glistening raiment, who gently spoke as follows : "I am your guardian angel, and am *counting the steps which you take for Christ's poor.*"'

The children understood the drift of it as well as you or I, reader ! and this is a sample of their daily talk. Their reverence for age is also a striking and touching characteristic. The poorest beggar is addressed by them as 'tio' or 'tia,' answering to our 'daddy' or 'granny ;' and should one pass their cottage as they are sitting down to their daily meal, they always rise and offer him a place, and ask him to say grace for them, 'echar la bendicion.' They are indeed a most loveable race, and their very pride increases one's respect for them. Often in their travels did one of the party lose her way, either in going to some distant church in the early morning, or in visiting the sick; and often was she obliged to have recourse to her bad Spanish to be put in the right road. An invariable courtesy, and generally an insistence on accompanying her home, was the result. But if any money or fee were offered for the service, the indignant refusal, or, still worse, the *hurt* look which the veriest child would put on at what it considered the height of insult and unkindness, very soon cured her of renewing the attempt.

Another touching trait in their character is their intense reverence for the Blessed Sacrament. In the great ceremonies of the church, or when It is passing down the street to a sick person, the same veneration is shown. One day, one of the English ladies was buying some photographs in a shop, and the tradesman was explaining to her the different prices and sizes of each, when, all of a sudden, he stopped short, exclaiming: 'Sua Maestà viene!' and leaving the astonished lady at the counter, rushed out of his shop-door. She, thinking it was the royalties, who were then at the Alcazar, went out too to look, when, to her pleasure and surprise, she saw the shopman and all the rest of the world, gentle and simple, kneeling reverently in the mud before the messenger of the Great King, who was bearing the Host to a dying man. On the day when It is carried processionally to the hospitals (one of which is the first Sunday after Easter), every window and balcony is 'parata,' or hung with red, as in Italy at the passage of the Holy Father; everyone throws flowers and bouquets on the baldachino, and that to such an extent that the choir-boys are forced to carry great clothes-baskets to receive them : the people declare that the very horses kneel! The Feast of Corpus Christi was unfortunately not witnessed by our travellers. Calderon, in his 'Autos Sacramentales,' speaking of it, says :—

Que en el gran dia de Dios,
Quien no está loco, no es cuerdo !

Here is indeed 'a voice from the land of Faith.' The choir on the occasion dance before the Host a dance so solemn, so suggestive, and so peculiar, that no one who has witnessed it can speak of it without emotion. Fernan Caballero talked much also of the great purity of morals among the

K

peasantry. Infanticide, that curse of England, is *absolutely unknown in Spain*; whether from the number of foundling hospitals, or from what other reasons, we leave it to the political economists to discover. A well-known Spanish writer describes the women as having 'Corazones delectos, minas de amores,' and being ' puros y santos modelos de esposas y de madres.' (Exceptional hearts, mines of love, and being pure and holy models of wives and mothers.) They are also wonderfully cleanly, both in their houses and their persons. There are never any bad smells in the streets or lodgings. Fleas abound from the great heat; but no other vermin is to be met with either in the inns, or beds, or in visiting among the sick poor, in all of which they form a marked contrast to the Italian peasantry, and, I fear we must add, to the English !

Their courtesy towards one another is also widely different from the ordinary gruff, boorish intercourse of our own poor people ; and the very refusal to a beggar, ' Perdone, Usted, por Dios, hermano !'* speaks of the same gentle consideration for the feelings of their neighbours which characterises the race and emanates from that divine charity which dwells not only on their

---

* 'Forgive me, for the love of God, brother!'

lips but in their hearts. One peculiarity in their conversation has not yet been alluded to, and that is their passion for proverbs. They cannot frame a sentence without one, and they are mostly such as illustrate the kindly, trustful, pious nature of the people. '*Haz lo bien, y no mira á quien.*' (Do good, and don't look to whom.) '*Quien no es agradecido, no es bien nacido.*' (He who is not courteous is not well born.) '*Cosa cumplida solo en la otra vida.*' (The end of all things is only seen in the future life.) And so on *ad infinitum.*

No description of Seville would be complete without mention of the 'patio,' so important a feature in every Andalusian house; and no words can be so good for the purpose as those of Fernan Caballero, which we translate almost literally from her 'Familia de Alvareda.'

'The house was spacious and scrupulously clean; on each side of the door was a bench of stone. In the porch hung a little lamp before the image of our Lord, in a niche over the entrance, according to the Catholic custom of placing all things under holy protection. In the middle was the " patio," a necessity to the Andalusian; and in the centre of this spacious court, an enormous orange-tree raised its leafy head from its robust and clean trunk. For an

infinity of generations had this beautiful tree
been a source of delight to the family. The
women made tonic concoctions of its leaves, the
daughters adorned themselves with its flowers,
the boys cooled their blood with its fruits, the
birds made their home in its boughs. The rooms
opened out of the "patio," and borrowed their
light from thence. This "patio" was the centre
of all—the "home," the place of gathering when
the day's work was over. The orange-tree loaded
the air with its heavy perfume, and the waters of
the fountain fell in soft showers on the marble
basin, fringed with the delicate maiden-hair fern;
and the father, leaning against the tree, smoked
his "cigarro de papel;" and the mother sat at her
work; while the little ones played at her feet, the
eldest resting his head on a big dog, which lay
stretched at full length on the cool marble slabs.
All was still, and peaceful, and beautiful.'

CHAPTER VII.

THE excursions in the neighbourhood of Seville are full of beauty and interest of various kinds. One of the first undertaken by our travellers was to the ruins of Italica, the ancient Seville, formerly an important Roman city, and the birthplace of Trajan and of Adrian. In the church, half convent and half fortress, are two very fine statues of St. Isidore and St. Jerome, by Montanés. Here St. Isidore began his studies. He was hopelessly dull and slow, and was tempted to give up the whole thing in despair, when one day, being in a brown study, his eye fell on an old well, the marble sides of which were worn into grooves by the continual friction of the cord which let down the bucket. 'If a cord can thus indent marble,' he said to himself, 'why should not constant study and perseverance make an impression on my mind?' His resolution was taken, and he became the light of his age and country. The well which gave him this useful lesson is still shown near the south door of the church. Here also is the monument of Doña Uraca Osorio, a lady who was burnt to death by order of King Pedro the Cruel, for having resisted his addresses. The flames having consumed the lower part of her dress, her faithful maid rushed into the fire, and died in endeavouring to conceal her mistress. In the sacristy is a very curious Byzantine picture of the Virgin. Leaving the church, our party went on to the amphitheatre, which has recently been excavated, and must have contained ten or twelve thousand people. A fine mosaic has lately been discovered, which evidently formed part of the ancient pavement. The custode was a character, and lived in a primitive little cabin at the entrance of the circus : a moss bed and a big cat seemed the only furniture. He was very proud of his tiny garden, poor old man! and of his wall-flowers, of which he gave the ladies a large bunch, together with a few silver coins which had been dug up in the excavations.

On their way home they passed by a cemetery in which was a very beautiful, though simple,

marble cross. On it were engraved these three
lines :—

Creo en Dios.
Espero en Dios.
Amo á Dios.

It was the grave of a poor boy, the only son of a
widow. He was not exactly an idiot, but what
people call a 'natural.' Good, simple, humble,
everyone loved him ; but no one could teach
him anything. His intelligence was in some way
at fault. He could remember nothing. In vain
the poor mother put him first to school, and then
to a trade ; he could not learn. At last, in despair,
she took him to a neighbouring monastery, and
implored the abbot, who was a most charitable
holy man, to take him in and keep him as a lay
brother. Touched by her grief, the abbot con-
sented, and the boy entered the convent. There,
all possible pains were taken with him by the
good monks to give him at least some ideas of
religion ; but he could remember nothing but
these three sentences. Still, he was so patient,
so laborious, and so good, that the community
decided to keep him. When he had finished his
hard out-of-door work, instead of coming in to
rest, he would go straight to the church, and there
remain on his knees for hours. 'But what does he

do ?' exclaimed one of the novices. 'He does not know how to pray. He neither understands the office, nor the sacraments, nor the ceremonies of the Church.' They therefore hid themselves in a side chapel, close to where he always knelt, and watched him when he came in. Devoutly kneeling, with his hands clasped, his eyes fastened on the tabernacle, he did nothing but repeat over and over again : 'Creo en Dios ; espero en Dios ; amo á Dios.' One day he was missing : they went to his cell, and found him dead on the straw, with his hands joined and an expression of the same ineffable peace and joy they had remarked on his face when in church. They buried him in this quiet cemetery, and the abbot caused these words to be graven on his cross. Soon, a lily was seen flowering by the grave, where no one had sown it ; the grave was opened, and the root of the flower was found in the heart of the orphan boy.*

Another morning our party visited the Cartucha, the once magnificent Carthusian convent, with its glorious ruined church and beautiful and extensive orange-gardens. Now all is deserted. The only thing remaining of the church is a fine west wall and rose-window, with a chapel which the proprietor has preserved for the use of his workpeople, and in the choir of which are some

* This anecdote is from the lips of Ferman Caballero.

finely carved wooden stalls : the rest have been
removed to Cadiz, where they form the great
ornament of the cathedral. Here and there are
some fine ' azulejos,' and a magnificently carved
doorway, speaking of glories long since departed.
This convent, once the very centre of all that was
most cultivated and literary in Spain, a museum
of painting, architecture, and sculpture, is now
converted into a porcelain manufactory, where
a good-natured Englishman has run up a tall
chimney, and makes ugly cheap pots and pans to
suit the taste and pockets of the Sevillians. Oh
for this age of ' progress ' ! It is fair to say that
the proprietor, who kindly accompanied the party
over the building, and into the beautiful gardens, and to the ruined pagoda or summer-house,
lamented that no encouragement was given by
the Spanish nobles of the present day to any
species of taste or beauty in design, and that his
attempts to introduce a higher class of china, in
imitation of Minton's, had met with decided
failure; no one would buy anything so dear.
They had imported English workmen and mo-
dellers in the first instance ; but he said that the
Spaniards were apt scholars, and had quickly
learned the trade, so that his workmen are now
almost exclusively from the country itself. The
only pretty thing our travellers could find, and

which was kindly presented to one of the party, was one of the cool picturesque-shaped bottles made, like the 'goolehs' of Egypt, of porous clay, which maintains the coldness and freshness of any liquid poured into it.

Among the many charming expeditions from Seville, is one to Castilleja (the village before alluded to as the scene of the death of Fernan Cortes), through the fertile plains and vineyards of Aljarafa. Here begins the region which the Romans called the Gardens of Hercules. It produces one of the best and rarest wines in Spain : the plants having been originally brought from Flanders by a poor soldier named Pedro Ximenes, who discovered that the Rhine vines, when transplanted to the sunny climate of Andalusia, lose their acidity, and yield the luscious fruit which still bears his name. In the centre of this fertile plain stands a small house and garden, to which is attached one of those tales of crime, divine vengeance, and godlike forgiveness, which are so characteristic of the people and country. About twenty years ago it was inhabited by a family consisting of a man named Juan Pedro Alfaro, with his wife, and a son of nineteen or twenty. Their quiet and peaceable lives were spent in cultivating their vineyard and selling its

produce in the neighbouring town. They were
good and respectable people, living in peace with
their neighbours, and perfectly contented with
their occupation and position. One thing only
was felt as a grievance. A lawyer, of the character of the 'Attorney Case' in our childhood's
story, had lately started an obnoxious new tax on
every cargo of wine brought into the city; and
this tax, being both unjust and illegal, they resolved to dispute. One day, therefore, when the
good man and his son were driving their mules
to market with their fruity burden, they were
stopped by the attorney, who demanded the usual
payment. The younger man firmly, but respect-
fully, refused, stating his reasons. The attorney
tried first fair words, and then foul, without
effect, upon which he vowed to be revenged.
The son, pointing to his Albacetan poniard, on
which was the inscription, 'I know how to de-
fend my master,' defied his vengeance; and so
they parted.

But never again was the poor wife and mother's
heart gladdened by the sight of their returning
faces. In vain she waited, hour after hour, that
first terrible evening. The mules returned, but
masterless. Then, beside herself with fear, the
poor woman rushed off to the town to make

enquiries as to their fate. No one knew anything further than that they had been at Seville
the day before, had sold their wine for a good
price, and been seen, as usual, returning cheer-
fully home. She then went to the Audiencia, or
legal supreme court of the city, where the ma-
gistrates, touched by her tale, and alarmed also
at the disappearance of the men, who were known
throughout the country for their high character
and respectability, caused a rigorous search to
be made in the whole neighbourhood; but in
vain. No trace of them could be discovered.
By degrees, the excitement in the town on the
subject passed away, and the poor muleteers
were forgotten; but in the heart of the widowed
mother there could be no rest and no peace.
The mystery in which their fate was involved
was so inexplicable that the hope of their return, however faint, would not die out; and for
twenty years she spent her life and her substance in seeking for her lost loved ones. At
last, reduced to utter misery, and worn out both
in mind and body, she was forced to beg her
daily bread of the charity of the peasants: the
' bolsa de Dios,' as the people poetically call it,
a ' bolsa ' which, to do the Spaniards justice, is
never empty. The little children would bring

her eggs and pennies; the fathers and husbands would give her a corner by the 'brasero' in winter, or under the vine-covered trellis in summer; the wives and mothers knew what had brought her to such misery, and had ever an extra loaf or a dish of 'garbanzos' set aside for the 'Madre Ana,' as she was called by the villagers. She, humble, prayerful, hopeful, ever grateful for the least kindness, and willing in any way to oblige others, at last fell dangerously ill. The curé, who had been striving to calm and soothe that sorely tried soul, was one day leaving her cottage, when his attention was attracted by a crowd of people, with the mayor at their head, who were hurrying towards an olive wood near the village. He followed, and, to his horror, found that the cause of the sensation was the discovery of two human skeletons under an olive-tree, the finger of one of which was pointing through the earth to heaven, as if for vengeance. The mayor ordered the earth to be removed: the surgeon examined the bodies, and gave it as his opinion that they must have been dead many years. But on examining the clothes, a paper was found which a waterproof pocket had preserved from decay. The attorney, who was likewise present, seized it; but no sooner had his

eyes lighted on the words, than he fell backwards
in a swoon. 'What is the matter? what has he
read?' exclaimed the bystanders as with one
voice. 'It is a certificate such as used to be
carried by our muleteers,' exclaimed the mayor,
taking the paper from the lawyer's hand; and
opening it, he read out loud the following words:
'*Pass for Juan Pedro Alfaro.*'

Here, then, was the unravelling of the terrible
mystery: the men had evidently been murdered
on their way home. The attorney recovered
from his fainting fit, but fever followed, and in his
delirium he did nothing but exclaim: 'It is not
I!—my hands are free from blood. It is Juan
Caño and Joseph Salas.' These words, repeated
by the people, caused the arrest of the two men
named, who no sooner found themselves in the
hands of justice than they confessed their crime,
and described how, having been excited to do so
by the attorney, they had shot both Juan Alfaro
and his son, from behind some olive-trees, on
their way home from market, had robbed, and
afterwards buried them in the place where the
bodies had been found. Sentence of death was
passed upon the murderers, while the attorney
was condemned to hard labour for life, and to
witness, with a rope round his neck, the execu-

tion of his accomplices in the fatal deed. The poor 'Madre Ana' had hardly recovered from her severe illness when these terrible events transpired. The indignation of the peasantry, and their compassion for her, knew no bounds : they would have torn the attorney in pieces if they could. The widow herself, overwhelmed with grief at this confirmation of her worst fears, remained silent as the grave. At last, when those around her were breathing nothing but maledictions on the heads of the murderers, and counting the days to the one fixed for the execution of their sentence, she suddenly spoke, and asked that the curé should be sent for. He at once obeyed the summons. She raised herself in the bed with some effort, and then said : 'My father, is it not true that, if pardon be implored for a crime by the one most nearly related to the victims, the judges generally mitigate the severity of the punishment ?' He replied in the affirmative. 'Then to-morrow,' she replied, 'I will go to Seville.' 'God bless you! my daughter,' replied the old priest, much moved ; 'the pardon you have so freely given in your heart will be more acceptable to God than the deaths of these men.' A murmur of surprise and admiration, and yet of hearty approval, passed through the lips of the bystanders. The next day, mounted carefully by the peasants on their best mule, the poor widow arrived at the Audiencia. Her entrance caused a stir and an emotion in the whole court. Bent with age, and worn with sickness and misery, she advanced in front of the judges, who, seeing her extreme weakness, instantly ordered a comfortable chair to be brought for her. But the effort had been too much; she could not speak. The judge then addressing her, said : 'Señora, is it true that you are come to plead for the pardon of Juan Caño and Joseph Salas, convicted of the assassination of your husband and son? and also for the pardon of the lawyer, who, by his instigation, led them to commit the crime?' She bowed her head in token of assent. A murmur of admiration and pity spread through the court; and a relation of the lawyer's, who saw his family thus rescued from the last stage of degradation, eagerly bent forward, exclaiming : 'Señora, do not fear for your future. I swear that every want of yours shall henceforth be provided for.'

The momentary feebleness of the woman now passed away. She rose to her full height, and casting on the speaker a look of mingled indignation and scorn, exclaimed : 'You offer me payment for my pardon ? I do not *sell* the blood of my son ! '

No account of ' life in Seville ' would be complete without a bull-fight, ' corrida de toros ; ' and so one afternoon saw our travellers in a tolerably spacious loggia on the shady side of the circus, preparing, though with some qualms of conscience, to see, for the first time, this, the great national sport of Spain. The roof of the cathedral towered above the arena, and the sound of the bells just ringing for vespers made at least one of the party regret the decision which had led her to so uncongenial a place. But it was too late to recede. No one could escape from the mass of human beings tightly wedged on every side, all eager for the fight. Partly, perhaps, owing to the mourning and consequent absence of the court, there were very few ladies ; which it is to be hoped is also a sign that the ' corrida ' has no longer such attractions for them. Presently the trumpets sounded. One of the barriers which enclosed the arena was thrown open, and in came a procession of ' toreros,' ' banderilleros,' and ' chulos,' all attired in gay and glittering costumes, chiefly blue and silver, the hair of each tied in a net, with a great bow behind, and with tight pink silk stockings and

L

buckled shoes. With them came the 'picadores,' dressed in yellow, with large broad-brimmed hats and iron-cased legs, riding the most miserable horses that could .be seen, but which, being generally thoroughbred, arched their necks and endeavoured, poor beasts! to show what once they had been. They were blindfolded, without which they could not have been induced to face the bull. The procession stopped opposite the president's box, when the principal 'torero' knelt and received in his hat the key of the bull's den, which was forthwith opened; and now the sport began. A magnificent brownish-red animal dashed out into the centre of the arena, shaking his crest and looking round him as if to defy his adversaries, pawing the ground the while. The men were all watching him with intense eagerness. Suddenly the bull singled out one as his adversary, and made a dash at a 'bande-rillero' who was agitating a scarlet cloak to the left. The man vaulted over the wooden fence into the pit. The bull, foiled, and knocking his horns against the wooden palings with a force which seemed as if it would bring the whole thing down, now rushed at a 'picador' to the right, from whose lance he received a wound in the shoulder. But the bull, lowering his head, drove

his horns right into the wretched horse's entrails,
and, with almost miraculous strength, galloped
with both horse and rider on his neck round the
whole arena, finally dropping both, when the
'picador' was saved by the 'chulos,' but the horse
was left to be still further gored by the bull, and
then to die in agony on the sand. This kind of
thing was repeated with one after the other, till
the bull, exhausted and covered with lance-
wounds, paused as if to take breath. The 'banderilleros' chose this moment, and with great skill
and address advanced in front of him, with their
hands and arms raised, and threw forward ar-
rows, ornamented with fringed paper, which they
fixed into his neck. This again made him furious, and, in eager pursuit of one of his enemies,
the poor beast leapt out of the arena over the
six-feet high barrier into the very middle of the
crowded pit. The 'sauve qui peut' may be imagined; but no one was hurt, and the din raised
by the multitude seemed to have alarmed the bull,
who trotted back quietly into the circus by a
side-door which had been opened for the purpose. New came the exciting moment. The judge
gave the signal, and one of the most famous
'matadores,' Cuchares by name, beautifully dressed
in blue and silver, and armed with a short sharp

sword, advanced to give the *coup de grâce.* This requires both immense skill and great agility; and at this very moment, when our party were wound up to the highest pitch of interest and excitement, a similar scene had ended fatally for the 'matador' at Cadiz. But Cuchares seemed to play with his danger; and though·the bull, mad with rage, pursued him with the greatest fury, tearing his scarlet scarf into ribands, and nearly throwing down the wooden screens placed at the sides of the arena as places of refuge for the men when too closely pressed to escape in other ways, he chose a favourable moment, and leaping forward, dug his short sword right into the fatal spot above the shoulder. With scarcely a struggle, the noble beast fell, first on his knees, and then rolled over dead. The people cheered vociferously, the trumpets sounded. Four mules, gaily caparisoned, were driven furiously into the arena; the huge carcase, fastened to them by ropes, was dragged out, together with those of such of the horses as death had mercifully released, and then the whole thing began over again. Twenty horses and six bulls were killed in two hours and a half, and the more horrible the dis-embowelled state of the animals, the greater seemed the delight of the spectators. It is im-

possible, without disgusting our readers, to give
a truthful description of the horrible state of the
horses. One, especially, caused a sensation even
among the 'habitués' of the ring. He belonged
to one of the richest gentlemen in Seville, had
been his favourite hack, and was as well known
in the Prado as his master. Yet this gentleman had the brutality, when the poor beast's work
was ended, to condemn him to this terrible fate!
The gallant horse, disembowelled as he was,
would not die: he survived one bull after the
other, though his entrails were hanging in festoons
on their horns, and finally, when the gates were
opened to drag out the carcases of the rest, he
managed to crawl away also—and to drag himself
where? To the very door of his master's house,
which he reached, and where he finally laid down
and died. His instinct, unhappily wrong in this
case, had evidently made him fancy that *there*,
at any rate, he would have pity and relief from his
agony: for the wounds inflicted by the horns of
the bull are, it is said, horrible in their burning,
smarting pain. Fernan Caballero was with the
wife of a famous 'matador,' whose chest was trans-
fixed by the bull at the moment when, thinking
the beast's strength was spent, he had leant forward
to deal the fatal stroke. He lingered for some

hours, but in an agony which she said must have been seen to be believed. Generally speaking, however, such accidents to the men are very rare. Carlo Puerto, one of the 'picadores,' was killed last year by a very wary bull, who turned suddenly, and catching him on his horns in the stomach, ran with him in that way three times round the arena!—but that was the fault of the president, who had insisted on his attacking the bull in the centre of the ring, the 'picadores' always remaining close to the screen, so that their escape may be more easily managed. If the sport could be conducted, as it is said to be in Salamanca and in Portugal, without injury to the horses, the intense interest caused by a combat where the skill, intelligence, and agility of the man is pitted against the instinct, quickness, and force of the bull, would make it perhaps a legitimate as well as a most exciting amusement; but as it is at present conducted, it is simply horrible, and inexcusably cruel and revolting. It is difficult to understand how any woman can go to it a second time. The effect on the people must be brutalising to a frightful extent, and accounts in a great measure for their utter absence of feeling for animals, especially horses and mules, which they ill-use in a manner perfectly shocking to an

Englishman, and apparently without the slightest sense of shame.   But there is no indication of this sport becoming less popular in Spain.   Combats with 'novillos,' or young bulls, whose horns are tipped to avoid accidents, are a common amuse-' ment among the young aristocracy, who are said to bet frightfully on their respective favourites; and thus the taste is fostered from their cradles.

The programme, or play-bill, is given literally in the Appendix, together with an amusing version of the fight in the Spanish 'vernacular' of the 'Ring.'

CHAPTER VIII.

THE CHARITABLE INSTITUTIONS AND CONVENTS OF SEVILLE.

A FEW days after the Holy Week, our travellers decided on visiting some of the far-famed charitable institutions of Seville ; and taking the kind and benevolent Padre B—— as their interpreter, they went first to the Hospital del Sangre, or of the ' five Wounds,' a magnificent building of the sixteenth century, with a Doric façade 600 feet long, a beautiful portal, and a ' patio,' in the centre of which is the church, a fine building, built in the shape of a Latin cross, and containing one or two good Zurbarans. There are between 300 and 400 patients ; and in addition to the large wards, there are—what is so much needed in our great London hospitals, and which we have before alluded to at Madrid—a number of nicely-furnished little separate rooms for a higher class of patients, who pay about two shillings a day, and have both the skill of the doctors and

the tender care of the sisters of charity, instead
of being neglected in their own homes. There
was a poor priest in one of these apartments,
in another a painter, and in a third a naval
captain, a Swede, and so on. The hospital is
abundantly supplied with everything ordered by
the doctors, including wine, brandy, chickens, or
the like ; and in this respect is a great contrast
to that at Malaga, where the patients literally die
for want of the necessary extra diets and stimu-
lants which the parsimony of the administration
denies them. In each quadrangle is a nice garden, with seats and fountains, and full of sweet
flowers, where the patients, when well enough,
can sit out and enjoy the sunshine. There is not
the slightest *hospital smell* in any one of the
wards. The whole is under the administration
of the Spanish sisters of charity of St. Vincent de
Paul ; and knowing that, no surprise was felt at
the perfection of the ' lingerie,' or the admirable
arrangement and order of the hospital. They
have a touching custom when one of the patients is dying, and has received the viaticum, to
place above his head a special cross, so that he
may be left undisturbed by casual visitors. The
sisters have a little oratory upstairs, near the
women's ward, beautifully fitted up. An air of

refinement, of comfort, and of *home*, pervades the whole establishment.

Close to this hospital is the old tower where St. Hermengilde was put to death, on Easter eve, by order of his unnatural father, because he would not join the Arian heresy, or receive his paschal communion from the hands of an Arian bishop. This was in the sixth century : and is not the same persecution, and for·the same cause, going on in Poland in the nineteenth ?* The old Gothic tower still remains, and in it his close dungeon. A church has been built adjoining, but the actual prison remains intact. There are some good pictures in the church, especially a Madonna, by Murillo ; and a clever picture of St. Ignatius in his room, meditating on his conversion. There is also a fine statue of

* The manner in which, during this very last Easter, the poor Polish Catholics have been treated and forced to receive schismatical communions through a system of treachery unparalleled in the annals of the Church, is unfortunately not sufficiently known in England, where alone public opinion could be brought to bear on the instigators of such tyranny. The strife between Russia and Poland has ceased to be anything but a religious struggle : Russia is determined to quench Catholicism out of the land. But the cry of hundreds of exiled pastors of the flock is rising to heaven from the forests and mines of Siberia : in the Holy Sacrifice (offered in earthenware cups on common stones) they still plead for their people before the Throne of the Great Intercessor. And that cry and those prayers will be answered in God's own time and way.

St. Hermengilde himself, by Montañés, over the high altar. The good old priest who had the care of this church lived in a little room adjoining, like a hermit in his cell, entirely devoted to painting and to the 'culte' of his patron saint. St. Gregory the Great attributes to the merits of this martyr the conversion of his brother, afterwards King Recared, the penitence of his father, and the Christianising of the whole kingdom of the Visigoths in Spain.

From thence our travellers went on to the orphanage managed by the 'Trinitarian sisters.' The house was built in the last century, by a charitable lady, who richly endowed it, and placed 200 children there ; now, the government, without a shadow of right, has taken the whole of the funds of the institution, and allows them barely enough to purchase bread. The superior is in despair, and has scarcely the heart to go on with the work. She has diminished the number of the children, and has been obliged to curtail their food, giving them neither milk nor meat except on great festivals. But for the intervention of the Duc de Montpensier, and other charitable persons, the whole establishment must long since have been given up. There are twenty-four sisters. The children work and embroider beautifully, and are trained to every kind of industrial occupation. From this orphanage our party went to the Hospital for Women, managed by the sisters of the third order of St. Francis. It is one of the best hospitals in Seville. There are about 100 women, admirably kept and cared for, and a ward of old and incurable patients besides. The superior, a most motherly, loving soul, to whom everyone seemed much attached, took them over every part of the building. She has a passion for cats, and beautiful 'Angoras' were seen basking in the sun in every window-sill.

This hospital, like the orphanage, is a private foundation; but the government has given notice that they mean to appropriate its funds, and the poor sisters are in terror lest their supplies should cease for their sick. It is a positive satisfaction to think that the government which has dealt in this wholesale robbery of the widow and orphan is not a bit the better for it. One feels inclined to exclaim twenty times a day: 'Thy money perish with thee!'

But of all the charitable institutions of Seville, the finest is the Caridad, a magnificent hospital, or rather 'asilo,' for poor and incurable patients, nursed and tended by the Spanish sisters of St. Vincent de Paul. It was founded in the seven-

teenth century, by Don Miguel de Mañara, a man
eminent for his high birth and large fortune, and
one of the knights of Calatrava, an order only
given to people whose quarterings showed no-
bility for several generations. He was in his
youth the Don Juan of Seville, abandoning himself to every kind of luxury and excess, although
many strange warnings were sent to him, from
time to time, to arrest him in his headlong, down-
ward course. On one occasion especially, he
had followed a young and apparently beautiful
figure through the streets and into the cathedral, where, regardless of the sanctity of the
place, he insisted on her listening to his addresses.
What was his horror, on her turning round, in
answer to his repeated solicitations, when the
face behind the mask proved to be that of a
skeleton ! So strongly was this circumstance
impressed on his mind, that he caused it afterwards to be painted by Valdés, and hung in the
council-room of the hospital. Another time,
when returning from one of his nocturnal orgies,
he lost his way, and, passing by the Church of
Santiago, saw, to his surprise, that the doors
were open, the church lit, and a number of priests
were kneeling with lighted tapers round a bier
in perfect silence. He went in and asked 'whose

was the funeral?' The answer of one after the other was: 'Don Miguel de Mañara.' Thinking this a bad joke, he approached the coffin, and hastily lifted up the black pall which covered the features of the dead. To his horror, he recognised himself. This event produced a complete change in his life. He resolved to abandon his vicious courses, and marry, choosing the only daughter of a noble house, as much noted for her piety as for her beauty. But God had higher designs in store for him, and after a few years spent in the enjoyment of the purest happiness, his young wife died suddenly. In the first violence of his grief, Don Miguel thought but of escaping from the world altogether, and burying himself in a monastery. But God willed it otherwise. There was at that time, on the right bank of the Guadalquiver, a little hermitage dedicated to St. George, which was the resort of a confraternity of young men who had formed themselves into brothers of charity, and devoted themselves to the care of the sick and dying poor. Don Diego Mirafuentes was their 'hermano mayor,' or chief brother, and being an old friend of Don Miguel's, invited him to stay with him, and, by degrees, enlisted all his sympathies in their labours of love. He desired to be enrolled in their confraternity, but his repu-

tation was so bad, that the brotherhood hesitated
to admit him; and when at last they yielded,
determined to put his sincerity and humility to
the test by ordering him to go at once from door
to door throughout Seville (where he was so well
known) with the bodies of certain paupers, and
to crave alms for their interment. Grace triumphed over all natural repugnance to such a
task; and with his penitence had come that natural thirst for penance which made all things
appear easy and light to bear, so that very soon
he became the leader in all noble and charitable
works.

Finding that an asylum or home was sadly
needed in winter for the reception of the houseless
poor, he purchased a large warehouse, which he
converted into rooms for this purpose; and by
dint of begging, got together a few beds and
necessaries, so that by the Christmas following
more than 200 sick or destitute persons were here
boarded and lodged. From this humble beginning arose one of the most magnificent charitable institutions in Spain. The example of Don
Miguel, his burning charity, his austere self-
denial, his simple faith, won all hearts. Money
poured in on every side; every day fresh candidates from the highest classes pleaded for admis-

sion into the confraternity. It was necessary to
draw up certain rules for their guidance, and this
work was entrusted to Don Miguel, who had
been unanimously elected as their superior. Nowhere did his wisdom, prudence, and zeal appear
more strongly than in these regulations, which
still form the constitutions of this noble foundation. Defining, first, the nature of their work—
the seeking out and succouring the miserable,
nursing the sick, burying the dead, and attend-
ing criminals to their execution—he goes on to
insist on the value of personal service, both private and public ; on the humility and self-abnegation required of each brother ; that each, on
entering the hospital, should forget his rank, and
style himself simply ' servant of the poor,' kissing
the hand of the oldest among the sufferers, and
serving them as seeing Jesus Christ in the persons of each. The notices of certain monthly
meetings and church services which formed part
of the rule of the community were couched in the
following terms :—' This notice is sent you lest
you should neglect these holy exercises, which
may be the last at which God will allow you to
assist.' Sermons and meditations on the Passion
of our Lord, and on the nearness of death and of
eternity, formed the principal religious exercises

of the confraternity; in fact, the Passion is the
abiding devotion of the order.

His hospital built, and his poor comfortably
housed and cared for, Don Miguel turned his
attention to the church, which was in ruins. A
letter of his, still extant, will show the difficulties
which he had to overcome in this undertaking.
'We had hoped,' he writes, 'that one of our
brothers, who was rich and childless, would have
given us something to begin the restoration; but
he died without thinking of the church, and so
vanished our golden hopes, as they always will
when we put our trust in human means to ac-
complish God's ends. I was inclined to despond
about it; when, the next morning, at eight
o'clock, a poor beggar named Luis asked to
speak to me. "My wife is just dead," he said.
"She sold chestnuts on the Plaza, and realised
a little sum of eighty ducats. To bury her I
have spent thirty: fifty remain; they are all I
have; but I bring them to you that you may
lay the first stone of the new church. I want
nothing for myself but a bit of bread, which I
can always beg from door to door." ' Don Miguel
refused; the beggar insisted, and so the church
was begun: and the story spread, and half a
million of ducats were poured into the laps of

the brothers ; but, as Mañara added, 'the first
stone was laid by God Himself in the " little all "
of the poor beggar.' *   This church was filled in
1680 with the chefs-d'œuvre of Murillo and of
Valdés Leal : an autograph letter from the great
religious painter is still shown in the Sala Capitular of the hospital, asking to be admitted as a
member of the confraternity. 'Our Saviour as a
Child ; ' ' St. John and the Lamb ; ' ' San Juan de
Dios with an Angel ; ' the 'Miracle of the Loaves
and Fishes ; ' but, above all, 'Moses striking the
Rock,' called 'La Sed' (so admirably is *thirst* represented in the multitudes crowding round the
prophet in the wilderness), were the magnificent
offerings of the new 'brother' towards the deco-
ration of God's house and the cause of charity.
Equally striking, but more painful in their choice
of subjects, are the productions of Valdés, especially a 'Dead Bishop,' awful in its contrast of
gorgeous robes with the visible work of the
worms beneath, and of which Murillo said 'that
he could not look at it without holding his
nose.' Other pictures by Murillo formerly decorated these walls ; but they were stolen by the

---

* How often, when buying chestnuts of one of the old women in
the Plaza of the Caridad, did the recollection of this story come
into the mind of our traveller !

French, and afterwards sold to English collectors,
the Duke of Sutherland and Mr. Tomline being
among the purchasers. After the church, the
most remarkable thing in the Caridad is the ' patio,' divided into two by a double marble colonnade. Here the poor patients sit out half the
day, enjoying the sunshine and the flowers. On
the wall is the following inscription, from the pen
of Mañara himself, but which loses in the translation :—' This house will last as long as God
shall be feared in it, and Jesus Christ be served
in the persons of His poor. Whoever enters here
must leave at the door both avarice and pride.'

The cloisters and passages are full of texts and
pious thoughts, but all associated with the two
ideas ever prominent in the founder's mind—
charity and death. Over what was his own cell
is the following, in Spanish :—' What is it that we
mean when we speak of Death ? It is being free
from the body of sin, and from the yoke of our
passions : therefore, to live is a bitter death, and
to die is a sweet life.'

The wards are charmingly large and airy, and
lined with gay ' azulejos.' The kitchen is large
and spacious, with a curious roof, supported by a
single pillar in the middle. Over the president's
chair, in the Sala Capitular, is the original

portrait of Don Miguel Mañara, by his friend
Valdés Leal, and, at the side, a cast taken of his
face after death, presented to the confraternity
by Vicentelo de Leca. Both have the same expression of dignity and austerity, mingled with
tenderness, especially about the mouth ; and the
features have a strong resemblance to those of
the great Condé. He died on May 19, 1679,
amidst the tears of the whole city, being only
fifty-three years of age : but a nature such as his
could not last long. A very interesting collection of his letters is still shown in the hospital,
and his life has been lately admirably translated
into French by M. Antoine de Latour.

The ' Sacré Cœur ' have established themselves
lately in Seville, through the kindness of the
Marquesa de V——, and are about to open a ladies' school—which is very much needed—on the
site of a disused Franciscan convent. The archbishop has given them the large church adjoining
the convent ; and it was almost comical to see the
three or four charming sisters, who are beginning this most useful and charitable work, singing
their benediction *alone* in the vast chancel, until
the building can be got ready for the reception of
their pupils.

Another convent visited by the ladies of the

party was that of Sta. Ines, which stands in a
narrow street near the Church of S. Felipe Neri.
The great treasure of this convent is the body of
Sta. Maria Coronel, which remains as fresh and
as life-like as if she had died but yesterday. Her
history is a tragical one. Pedro the Cruel, falling
madly in love with her great beauty, condemned
her husband, who was governor of the Balearic
Islands, to an ignominious death ; but then, with
a refinement of cruelty, promised his pardon to
his wife on condition that she would yield to his
passion. Maria Coronel, preferring death to dis-
honour, permitted the execution of her husband,
and fled for refuge to this convent, where the
king, violating all rights, human and divine, pursued her. One night he penetrated into her cell.
Maria, seeing no other mode of escape, seized the
lamp which burnt on the table before her, and
poured the boiling oil over her face, thus destroy-
ing her beauty for ever. The king, enraged and
disappointed, relinquished his suit ; and the poor
lady lived and died in the convent. In the library of the University is an ancient MS. describing Pedro the Cruel as ' tall, fair, good-looking,
and full of spirit, valour, and talent !' but his exe-
crable deeds speak for themselves. The curious
thing is, that the marks of the boiling oil are as

clearly seen on Maria Coronel's face now as on the day when the heroic deed was committed. The sisters of this convent are dressed in blue, with a long black veil, and their cloisters contain some very curious pictures and relics.

The most interesting visit, however, paid by one of the party in Seville, was to the strictly enclosed convent of Sta. Teresa, to enter which the English lady had obtained special Papal permission. Of the sorrows and perils which St. Theresa experienced in founding this house, she herself speaks in writing to her niece, Mary of Ocampo :—' I assure you that of all the persecutions we have had to endure, none can bear the least comparison with what we have suffered at Seville.'* Suffering from violent fever, calumniated by one of her own postulants, denounced to the Inquisition, persecuted incessantly by the fathers of the mitigated rule, with no prospect of buying a house, and no money for the purchase,

---

* For both this and other quotations regarding St. Theresa's foundations, the writer is indebted to the charming life of the saint published by Hurst & Blackett in 1865, and which, from its wonderful truth and accuracy, is a perfect handbook to anyone visiting the Carmelite convents of Spain. She trusts that its author will forgive her for having, often unintentionally, used her actual expressions in speaking of places and of things, from the impossibility of their being described by an eye-witness in any other manner.

the saint could yet find courage to add : 'Notwithstanding all these evils, my heart is filled with joy. What blessed things are peace of conscience and liberty of soul !' It reminds one of another occasion, when it was necessary to begin a foundation which was to cost a great deal of money, and the saint had but twopence-halfpenny. 'Never mind,' she replied, courageously, ' Twopence-halfpenny and Theresa are nothing ; but twopence-halfpenny and God are everything !' and the work was accomplished. In the case of the Seville house her patience and faith met with a like reward. On the Feast of the Ascension, 1576, the Blessed Sacrament was placed in the chapel of the new convent by the archbishop himself, accompanied by all his clergy, who wished to make public amends to St. Theresa and her nuns for the persecutions they had endured ; and when Theresa knelt to ask for his pastoral benediction, the archbishop, in the presence of all the people, knelt to ask for hers in return, thus testifying to the high estimation in which he held both her and her work.

It was this convent, untouched since those days of trial, which our visitors now entered. There are twenty-two sisters, of whom three are novices, and their rule is maintained in all its primitive severity. They keep a perpetual fast, living chiefly on the dried 'cabala,' or stockfish, of the country, and only on festivals and at Easter-tide allowing themselves eggs and milk.

They have no beds, only a hard mattress, stuffed with straw ; this, with an iron lamp, a pitcher of water, a crucifix, and a discipline, constitutes the only furniture of each cell, all of which are alike. One or two common prints were pasted on the walls, and over the doors hung various little ejaculations : 'Jesu, superabundo gaudio ;' 'O crux ! ave, spes unica !' 'Domine, quid me vis facere ?' or else a little card in Spanish, like the following, which the English lady carried off with her as a memorial :—

> Aplaca, mi Dios, Tu ira,
> Tu justicia y Tu rigor.
> Por los ruegos de María,
> Misericordia, Señor !
> Santo Dios, Santo fuerte, Santo inmortal,
> Liberanos, Señor, de todo mal.

At the refectory, each sister has an earthenware plate and jug, with a wooden cover, an earthenware salt-cellar, and a wooden spoon. Opposite the place of the superior is a skull, the only distinction. They are allowed no linen except in sickness, and wear only a brown mantle and white serge scapular, with a black veil, which covers them from head to foot. They are rarely allowed to walk in the garden, or to go out in the corridor in the sun to warm themselves. Their house is like a cellar, cold and damp; and they have no fires. Even at recreation they are not allowed to sit, except on the floor; and silence is rigidly observed, except for two hours during the day. They have only five hours' sleep, not going to bed till half-past eleven, on account of the office. At eleven, one of the novices seizes the wooden clapper (or crecella), which she strikes three times, pronouncing the words : ' Praise be to our Lord Jesus Christ, and to the Blessed Virgin Mary, His Mother ; my sisters, let us go to matins to glorify our Lord.' Then they go to the choir, singing the Miserere. They are called again in the same manner at half-past four by a sister who chaunts a verse in the Psalms. At night, a sentence is pronounced aloud, to serve as meditation. It is generally this :—

My sisters, think of this : a little suffering, and then an eternal recompense.

They see absolutely *no one*, receiving the Holy Communion through a slit in the wall. The English lady was the first person they had seen face to face, or with lifted veils, for twelve years

They play the organ of the chapel, which is a public one, though they themselves are entirely invisible; and they are not even allowed to see the altar, which is concealed by a heavy black curtain drawn across the grating looking into the church. They have an image of their great foundress, the size of life, dressed in the habit of the order, and to her they go night and morning and salute her, as to a mother. Their convent is rich in relics, beautiful pictures, and crucifixes, brought in by different religious, especially the Duchesse de Bega, who became a Carmelite about fifty years ago. But their chief treasure is an original picture of St. Theresa, for which she sat by command of the archbishop, and which has lately been photographed for the Duc de Montpensier. It is a very striking and beautiful face, but quite different from the conventional representations of the saint. When it was finished, she looked at it, and exclaimed naively: 'I did not know I was grown so old or so ugly!' There is also in this sacristy a very beautiful Morales of the 'Virgin and a Dead Christ,' and a curious portrait of Padre Garcia, the saint's confessor. Upstairs, in her own cell, they have her cloak and shoes, and the glass out of which she drank in her last illness, and which is in this shape: ⑂. The stranger was courteously made to drink out of it also, and then to put on the saint's cloak, in which she was told 'to kneel and pray for her heart's desire, and it would be granted to her.'

But the most interesting thing in the convent is the collection of MSS. They have the whole of the 'Interior Mansion,' written in her own firm and beautiful handwriting, with scarcely an erasure ; besides quantities of her letters and answers from St. John of the Cross, from St. John of Avila, from Padre Garcia, and a multitude of others. The superior is elected every three years, and the same one cannot be re-elected till three years have elapsed. They require a 'dot' of 8,000 reals, or about a hundred pounds ; but their number is full, and several candidates are now waiting their turn for admission. The government has taken what little property they once had, and gives them at the rate of a peseta (two reals) a day, so that, poor as their food is, they are often on the verge of starvation.

It was with a feeling almost of relief that the English lady found herself once more in the sunshine outside these gloomy walls ; yet those who lived within them seemed cheerful and happy, and able to realise in the fullest degree, without any external aid, those mysteries of Divine love and that beauty of holiness which, to our weaker faith, would seem impossible when deprived of all sight of our Lord in His tabernacle or in His glorious creations. We are tempted to ask, why it is that convents of this nature are so repugnant to English taste ? Everyone is ready to appreciate those of the sisters of charity. People talk of their good deeds, of the blessing they are in the hospitals, of the advantages of united work, &c., &c. ; but as for the enclosed orders, ' They wish they were all abolished.' ' What is the good of a set of women shutting themselves up and *doing nothing* ? ' Reader, *do* they ' do nothing ' ? We will not speak of the schools; of the evening classes for working women ; of the preparations for first communions and confirmations; of the retreats within their sheltering walls for those of us who, wearied with this world's toil and bustle, wish to pause now and then and gain breath for the daily fight, and take stock, as it were, of our state before God. These, and other works like these, form almost invariably a very important portion of the daily occupation of the cloistered orders. But we will dismiss the thoughts of any external work, and come to the highest and noblest part of their vocation. What is it that is to ' move moun-

tains ?' What is it that, over and over again
in Holy Scripture, has saved individuals, and
cities, and nations ? Is it not united intercessory prayer ? Is it nothing to us, in the whirl
and turmoil of this work-a-day life, that holy
hands should ever be lifted up for us to the Great
Intercessor ? Is there no *reparation* needed for
the sins, and the follies, and the insults to the
Majesty of God, and to His Sacraments, and to
His Mother, which are ever going on in this
our native country ? Does it not touch the most
indifferent among us to think of our self-indulgence being, as it were, atoned for by their
self-denial ?—our pampered appetites by their
fasts and vigils ? It is true that our present
habits of life and thought lead to an obvious
want of sympathy with such an existence. It
has no public results on which we can look complacently, or which can be paraded boastfully.
Everything seems waste which is not visible ;
and all is disappointment which is not obvious
success. It is supernatural principles especially
which are at a discount in modern days ! Surely
the time will come when we shall judge these
things very differently ; when our eyes will be
opened like the eyes of the prophet's servant ;
and we shall see from what miseries, from what

sorrows, we and our country have been preserved by lives like these, which save our Sodom, and avert God's righteous anger from His people.*

One more curious establishment was visited by our party at Seville before their departure, and that was the cigar manufactory, an enormous Government establishment, occupying an immense yellow building, which looks like a palace, and employing 1,000 men and 5,000 women. The rapidity with which the cigars are turned out by those women's fingers is not the least astonishing part. The workers are almost all young, and some very beautiful. They take off their gowns and their crinolines as soon as they come in, hanging them up in a long gallery, and take

* In a simple but touching French biography of a young English lady who lately died in the convent of the ' Poor Clares ' at Amiens, the writer's idea is far more beautifully expressed :—' A cette heure de la nuit, peut-être qu'une jeune fille du monde, martyre (sans couronne) de ses lois et de ses exigences, rentre chez elle, épuisée d'émotions et de fatigues. En longeant le mur du monastère et en entendant le son de la cloche qui appelle les recluses volontaires à la prière, elle se sera adressée cette question : "A quoi servent donc les religieuses ?" Je vais vous le dire : à expier. Après cette nuit de plaisir que vous venez de passer au théâtre ou au bal, viendra une autre nuit—nuit d'angoisses et de suprême douleur. Vous êtes là étendue sur votre couche de mort en face de l'éternité où vous allez entrer seule, et sans appui. Peut-être vous n'osez, ou vous ne pouvez prier ; mais quelqu'un a prié pour vous, et faisant violence au ciel, a obtenu ce que vous n'étiez pas digne d'espérer. Voilà à quoi servent les religieuses.'

the flowers out of their hair and put them in
water, so that they may be fresh when they come
out; and then work away in their petticoats
with wonderful zeal and good humour the whole
day long. The Government makes 90,000,000
reals a year from the profits of this establishment,
though the dearest cigar made costs but two-
pence!

And now the sad time came for our travellers
to leave Seville. In fact, the exorbitant prices
of everything at the hotel made a longer stay impossible, though it was difficult to say *what* it
was that they paid for: certainly *not food*; for ex-
cepting the chocolate and bread, which are invariably good throughout Spain, the dinners were
uneatable, the oil rancid, the eggs stale; even 'el
cocido,' the popular dish, was composed of indescribable articles, and of kids which seemed to
have died a natural death. One of the party, a
Belgian, exclaimed when her first dish of this
so-called meat was given her at Easter: 'Vraiment,
je crois que nous autres nous n'avons pas tant
perdu pendant le Carême!' An establishment has
lately been started by an enterprising peasant to
sell milk fresh from the cow, a great luxury in
Spain, where goat's milk is the universal substitute;
and four very pretty Alderneys are kept, stall-fed,

in a nice little dairy, 'à l'Anglaise,' at one corner
of the principal square, which is both clean and
tempting to strangers. At every corner of the
streets, water, in cool porous jars, is offered to
the passers-by, mixed with a sugary substance
looking like what is used by confectioners for
'meringues,' but which melts in the water and
leaves no trace. This is the universal beverage
of every class in Spain.

There is little to tempt foreigners in the shops
of Seville, and with the exception of photographs
and fans, there is nothing to buy which has any
particular character or 'chique' about it. The
fans are beautiful, and form, in fact, one of the
staple trades of the place; there is also a sweet
kind of incense manufactured of flowers, mixed
with resinous gums, which resembles that made
at Damascus. But the ordinary contents of the
shops look like the sweepings-out of all the
'quincaillerie' of the Faubourg St.-Denis.

It was on a more lovely evening than usual
that our travellers went, for the last time, to that
glorious cathedral. The sorrow was even greater
than what they had felt the year before in leaving
St. Peter's : for Rome one lives in hopes of seeing
again; Seville, in all human probability, never !
The services were over, but the usual proportion

of veiled figures knelt on the marble pavement, on which the light from those beautiful painted windows threw gorgeous colours. Never had that magnificent temple appeared more solemn or more worthy of its purpose ; one realised as one had never done before one's own littleness and God's ineffable greatness, mercy, and love. Still they lingered, when the inexorable courier came to remind them that the train was on the point of starting, and with a last prayer, which was more like a sob, our travellers left the sacred building. At the station all their kind Seville friends had assembled to bid them once more good-bye, and to re-echo kind hopes of a speedy return ; and then the train started, and the last gleam of sunshine died out on the tower of the Giralda.

N

CHAPTER IX.

THE ESCURIAL AND TOLEDO.

THE journey to Madrid was uneventful. One more day was spent in Cordova; once more they visited that glorious mosque; one more day and night was spent in wearisome diligences and stifling wayside stations, and then they found themselves again established in their old comfortable quarters in the ' Puerta del Sol.'

It was a relief to think that the ' lions ' of the place had been more or less visited, and that all they had to do was to return to the places of previous interest, and thoroughly enjoy them. The cold during their former visit had precluded their making any expeditions in the neighbourhood, which omission they now prepared to rectify. Spending the first few days in seeing their old friends, and obtaining letters of introduction from them, our travellers resolved that their first excursion should be to the Escurial.

A railroad is now open from Madrid which

passes by the palace; so at half-past six one morning they took their places in the train, which soon
carried them away from the cultivated environs
of the city to a country which, for desolation,
wildness, and grandeur, resembles the scenery at
Nicolosi in the ascent of Etna. In the midst of
this rugged mass of rocks and scrubby oak-trees,
the large gloomy Escurial rises up, under the
shadow, as it were, of the snowy jagged peaks
of the Sierra Guadarama, which forms its background. There is a picture of it, by Rubens, in
the gallery at Longford Castle, near Salisbury,
which gives the best possible idea of the complete
isolation of the great building itself, and of the
savage character of the whole of the surrounding
country.

Leaving the train, our party went to present
their letters to the principal, Padre G——, who
very kindly showed them everything most worth
seeing in the place. It is a gigantic pile of
masonry, built by Philip II. as a thanksgiving
for the success of the battle of St. Quentin, and
in the shape of a gridiron, being dedicated to
St. Laurence, on the day of whose martyrdom the
vow was made. 'Celui qui faisait un si grand
vœu doit avoir eu grande peur!' was the saying
of the Duke of Braganza; and the gloomy,

cold, grey character of the whole place is but the reflex of the king's temperament. He employed the famous architect Herrera, whose genius was, however, much cramped by the king's insistence on the shape being maintained. It was finished in 1584.

The Jeronimite monks have been scattered to the winds, and the convent has been turned into a college ; they have about 250 students. The church is large and solemn, but bare and uninviting, dismal and sombre, like all the rest. The choir is upstairs, with fine carved stalls, among which is that of Philip II., who always said office with the monks. The painted ceiling is by Luca Giordano. The choir-books are more than 200 in number, in virgin calf, and of gigantic size ; some of them are beautifully illuminated. At the back, in a small gallery, with a window looking on the great piazza below, is the famous white marble Christ, the size of life, by Benvenuto Cellini, given to Philip II. by the Grand Duke of Florence. On certain days it is exposed to the people from the window ; but wonderful as may be its anatomy, the expression is both painful and commonplace. Beneath the church is the famous crypt containing the bodies of all the kings and queens of Spain since Charles V., arranged in niches round the octagonal chapel. Each niche contains a black marble sarcophagus; the kings on the right, and the queens on the left. Here mass is always said on All Souls' Day, and on the anniversaries of their deaths. The present queen came once, and looked at the empty urn waiting for her, but did not repeat the experiment. 'I have come once of my own freewill,' she is supposed to have said, 'but the next time I shall be brought here without it.' It is a dismal resting-place; the damp, cold, slippery stairs by which you descend into it from the church seem to chill one's very blood, and the profound darkness, only lit up here and there by the flicker of the guide's torch, with the reverberation caused by the closing of the heavy iron door, fill the thoughts with visions of death, uncheered by hope, and of a prison rather than a grave. Ascending with a feeling of positive relief to the church above, Padre G—— took them into the sacristy, which is a beautiful long low room, with arabesque ceilings, and at the further end of which is a very fine picture by Coello, representing the apotheosis of the 'Forma,' or miraculous wafer: the heads are all portraits, and admirably executed. At the back is the little chapel or sanctuary where the 'Forma'

is kept and exhibited twice a year. Charles II.
erected the gorgeous altar with the following
inscription : —

En magni operis miraculum intra miraculum mundi, cœli miraculum consecratum.

The legend states that at the battle of Gorcum,
in 1525, the Zuinglian heretics scattered and
trampled on the Sacred Host, *which bled*; and
being gathered up and carefully preserved by
the faithful, was afterwards given by Rudolph II.
to Philip II., which event is represented in a
bas-relief. In this sacristy are also some vestments of which the embroidery is the most exquisite thing possible ; the faces of the figures are
like beautiful miniatures, so that it is difficult to
believe they are done in needlework.*

But the great treasures of this church are its
relics, of which the quantity is enormous. They
are arranged in gigantic cupboards or 'étagères,'
stretching from the floor to the ceiling, the doors
of which are carefully concealed by the pictures
which hang over them, above both the high
altar and the two side altars at the east end.
There are more than 7,000 relics, of which the

* In the Dominican convent of Stone, in Staffordshire, the same
exquisite work is now being reproduced; which proves that the
art is not, as is generally supposed, extinct.

most interesting are those of St. Laurence himself (his skull, his winding-sheet, the iron bars of
his gridiron, &c.), the head of St. Hermengilde,
sent to the king from Seville, and the arm and
head of St. Agatha. The reliquaries are also very
beautiful, some of them of very fine cinquecento
work. These are downstairs. Upstairs is a kind
of secret chapel, where there are some things
which were still more interesting to our travellers.
Here are four MS. books of St. Theresa's, all
written by her own hand; her 'Life,' written by
command of her confessor, Padre Báñez, with a
voucher of its authenticity from him at the end;
her 'Path of Perfection;' her 'Constitutions'
and 'Foundations;' also her inkstand and pen.
Her handwriting is more like a man's than a
woman's, and is beautifully clear and firm. There
is also a veil worked in a kind of crotchet by St.
Elizabeth of Hungary, and sent by her to St.
Margaret; a beautifully illuminated Greek missal, once belonging to St. Chrysostom; a pot
from Cana in Galilee; a beautifully carved ivory
diptych; the body of one of the Holy Innocents,
sent from Bethlehem; some exquisite ivory and
coral reliquaries, &c. From the church, our party
went up by a magnificent staircase to the library, which, though despoiled, like everything else

during the French invasion, still contains some invaluable books and MSS. There is an illuminated Apocalypse of the fourteenth century, most exquisitely painted on both sides; a very fine copy of the Koran; many other beautiful missals; and in a room downstairs, not generally shown to travellers, are some thousands of manuscripts, among which are a wonderful illuminated copy of the Miracles of the Virgin, in Portuguese and Gallego, of the eleventh century, most quaint and funny in design and execution; also a very curious illuminated book of chess problems, and other games, written by order of the king Alonso el Sabio. It is a library where one might spend days and days with ever-increasing pleasure, if it were not for the cold, which, to our travellers, fresh from the burning sun of Seville, seemed almost unendurable. The cloisters, refectory, and kitchens are all on the most magnificent scale. In the wing set aside for the private apartments of the royal family, but which they now rarely occupy, the thing most worth looking at is the tapestry, made in Madrid, at the Barbara factory (now closed), from drawings by Teniers and Goya. They are quite like beautiful paintings, both in expression and colour, though some of the subjects and scenes

are of questionable propriety. There is a suite
of small rooms with beautiful inlaid doors and
furniture; a few good pictures (among a good
deal of rubbish), especially one of Bosch, known
as that of 'The Dog and the Fly;' and a
very interesting gallery or corridor, covered with
frescoes, representing the taking of Granada on
the one side and the battle of St. Quentin on
the other, the victory of Lepanto occupying the
spaces at the two ends. These frescoes are very
valuable, both as portraits and as representing
the costumes and arms of the period. They were
said to be fac-simile copies of original drawings,
done on cloths on the actual spots. That of
St. Quentin was specially interesting to one of
the party, whose ancestor fought there, and in
whose house in England (Wilton Abbey) is still
shown the armour of Ann Conétable de Mont-
morency, of the Duc de Montpensier, of Admiral
Coligni, and of other French prisoners taken
by him in that memorable battle. Beyond this
gallery is the little business-room or study of
Philip II., with his chair, his gouty stool, his
writing-table, his well-worn letter-book, and two
old pictures, one of the Seven Deadly Sins, the
other an etching (of 1572) of the Virgin and
Saints. Out of this tiny den is a kind of recess,

with a window looking on the high altar in which he caused his couch to be laid when he was dying. The death-struggle was prolonged for fifty-three days of almost continuous agony, during which time he went on holding in his hand the crucifix which Charles V. had when he expired, and which is still religiously preserved. The gardens in front of this magnificent palace are very quaint and pretty, the beds being cut in a succession of terraces overlooking the plains below, and bordered with low box hedges cut in prim shapes, with straight gravel walks, beautiful fountains, and marble seats. But it is not difficult to understand why the poor queen prefers the sunny slopes of La Granja, or even the dullness of the green avenues of Aranjuez, to this gloomy pile, where the snow hardly ever melts in the cold shade of those inner courts, and where all the associations are of death in its most repulsive form. Above the Escurial, halfway up the mountain, is a rude seat of boulder stones, from whence it is said Philip II. used to watch the progress of the huge building.

Returning to the railway station, our travellers walked down the hill and through a pleasantly-wooded avenue to a little 'maisonnette' of the Infanta, built for Charles IV. when heir apparent.

and containing some beautiful ivories and Wedg-
woods. The gardens are pretty and bright, but
the whole thing is too small to be anything but a
child's toy. An accident on the line, somewhere
near Avila, detained our party for six mortal hours
at a wretched little wayside station, of which the
authorities flatly refused to put on a short special train, although there were a large number of
passengers, in addition to our travellers, waiting,
like them, to return to Madrid. But the Spanish
mind cannot take in the idea of anyone being in a
hurry. ' Ora !' ' Mañana !' (By and by ! To-morrow !) are the despairing words which meet one at
every turn in this country. In this instance, neither
horses nor carriages being procurable by which the
journey to Madrid (only twenty miles) could have
been accomplished with perfect facility by read,
our travellers had nothing left for it but to wait.
Patience, and such sleep as could be got on a hard
bench, were their only resource until one in the
morning, when the night express fortunately came
up, and, after some demur, agreed to take them
back to Madrid.

Too tired the following day to start early again
for Toledo, as they had intended, our party took
advantage of the kindness of the English minister
to see the queen's private library, which is in one

of the wings of the large but uninteresting modern palace. The librarian good-naturedly showed them some of the rarest of his treasures : among them is a beautiful missal, bound in shagreen, with lovely enamel clasps and exquisite illuminations, which had belonged to Queen Isabella of Castile ; her arms, Arragon on one side and Castile on the other, were worked into the illuminations on the cover. There was a still older missal illuminated in 1315, in which is found the first mention of *St. Louis* in the Kalendar. Here also are some of the first books printed in type, and a very fine MS. Greek copy of Aristotle.

Afterwards, they came to a distant room, where Dr. —— found what he had long sought for in vain—a quantity of the MS. letters of Gondomar, minister from Spain to our King James I., giving an amusing and gossiping account of people and things in England at that time. In this library is also a very curious and interesting MS. life of Cardinal Wolsey.

In the evening, one of the party paid a visit to the Papal Nunzio, Monsignor B——, a very kind, clever, and agreeable man, living in a quaint old house, with a snug library, in which hangs a pretty oil painting of Tyana, a picturesque country near Barcelona, of which he is archbishop. From him,

and from the venerable Monsignor S———, Bishop
of Daulia, she obtained certain letters of introduction to prelates and convents, which were
invaluable in her future tour, and procured for her
a kind and courteous welcome wherever she went.

The following morning, after a five o'clock mass
in the beautiful little chapel of the sisters of
charity, our travellers started for Toledo by rail,
passing by the Aranjuez, the 'Sans-Souci' of the
Spanish queen, where all the trees in Castile seem
to be collected for her special benefit, and where
the sight of the green avenues and fountains is a
real refreshment after the barren and arid features
of the rest of the country.

Toledo is a most curious and beautiful old town,
built on seven hills, like Rome. The approach to
it is by a picturesque bridge over the Tagus, which
rushes through a rent in the granite mountains
like a vigorous Scotch salmon-river, and encircles
the walls of the ancient city as with a girdle.
Passing under a fine old Moorish horse-shoe arched
gateway, a modern zigzag road leads up the steep
incline to the 'plaza,' out of which diverge a multitude of narrow tortuous streets, like what in
Edinburgh are called 'wynds,' as painful to walk
upon as the streets of Jerusalem. However, after
a vain attempt to continue in the Noah's Ark of

an omnibus which had brought them up the steep
hill from the station, and which grazed the walls
of the houses on each side from its width, our
travellers were compelled to brave the slippery
stones and proceed on foot. The little inn is as
primitive as all else in this quaint old town, where
everything seems to have stood still for the last
five centuries. Leaving their cloaks in the only
available place dignified by the name of ‘ Sala,’
and swallowing with difficulty some very nasty
coffee, they started off at once for the cathedral,
which stands in the heart of the city, surrounded
by convents and colleges, and with the archiepiscopal palace on the right. It is a marvel of Gothic
beauty and perfection. Originally a mosque, it
was rebuilt by Ferdinand, and converted by him
into a Christian church, being finished in 1490.
In no part of the world can anything be seen more
unique, more beautiful, or more effective than the
white marble screen, with its row of white angels
with half-folded wings, guarding the sanctuary of
the high altar, and standing out sharp and clear
against the magnificent dark background formed
by the arched naves and matchless painted glass,
which, in depth and brilliancy of colour and
beauty of design, exceeds even that of Seville.
‘ Shall you ever forget the blue eyes of those rose-

windows at Toledo?' exclaimed, months after, Dr.
—— to one of the party, who was dwelling with
him on the wonderful beauties of this matchless
temple.* The choir is exquisitely carved, both
above and below; the stalls divided by red marble
columns. Of the seventy stalls, half are carved
by Vigarny and half by Berruguete : each figure
of each saint is a study in itself. The high altar
is a perfect marvel of workmanship, the 'reredos'
or 'retablo' representing the whole life and passion
of our Lord. At the back is the wonderful marble
'trasparente,' which Ford calls an 'abomination of
the seventeenth century,' but which, when the sun
shines through it, is a marvel for effect of colour
and delicacy of workmanship. The Moorish altar
still remains at which Ferdinand and Isabella
heard mass after their conquest of the Saracens ;
and close to this altar is the spot pointed out by
tradition as the one where the Virgin appeared
to St. Ildefonso and placed the chasuble on his
shoulders. It is veiled off, with this inscription
on the pillar above :—

Adorabimus in loco ubi steterunt pedes ejus.

The fine bas-relief representing the miracle
was executed by Vigarny. Fragments of Sara-

* Incredible as it may seem, the guide-books state that there are
no less than 750 stained glass windows in this cathedral.

cenic art peep out everywhere, especially in the
Sala Capitular, or chapter room, of which the
doorway is an exquisite specimen of the finest
Moorish work, and the ceiling likewise. In this
chapter room are two admirable portraits of
Cardinal Ximenes and Cardinal Mendoza, said to
have been taken from life. The monuments in
the side chapels are very fine, especially one of
St. Ildefonso, whose body had been carried by the
Moors to Zamora, and was there discovered by a
shepherd, and brought back again; of Cardinal
Mendoza; of the Constable Alvaro de Luna; and
of several Spanish kings. Here also rests the
body of St. Leocadia, martyred in the persecution
under Diocletian, and to whom three churches
in Toledo are dedicated. During the wars with
the Moors, her body was removed to Italy, and
thence to Mons; but was brought back by
Philip II. to her native city, and is now in an
urn in the sacristy. At the west end of the
cathedral is a very curious chapel, where the
Muzarabic ritual is still used. This appears to
be to the Spaniards what the Ambrosian is to
the Milanese, and was established by Cardinal
Ximenes. The sacristy is a real treasure-house,
containing an exquisite tabernacle of gold brought
by Christopher Columbus, incensories, chalices,

crosses and reliquaries, in gold and enamel, and
'cristal de roche' (some given by Louis of France),
and the missal of St. Louis, of which the illuminations are as fine as any in the Vatican. The
robes, mantles, and ornaments of the Virgin are
encrusted with pearls and jewels. Cardinal Mendoza removed one side of the marble screen of
the high altar to make room for his own monument. In contrast to this, is another archbishop's
tomb, near the altar of the miraculous Virgin.
They wanted to give him a fine carved sepulchre,
and were discussing it in his presence a short
time before his death. He insisted on a simple
slab, with the following words :—

Hic jacet pulvis, cinis, nullus.

Close to the bénitière at the south entrance, is
a little marble slab attached to the pillar, and
on it a little soft leather cushion, which had
excited the curiosity of one of our party on entering. On returning for vespers, she found laid on
it a fine little baby, beautifully dressed, with a
medal round its neck, but quite dead ! One of
the canons explained to her that when the
parents were too poor to pay the expenses of
their children's funerals, they brought the little
bodies in this way for interment by the chapter.

o

The cloisters to the north of the cathedral are very lofty and fine, and decorated with frescoes ; and the doors with their magnificent bronze bas-reliefs, in the style of the Florence baptistery, and gloriously carved portals, are on a par with all the rest. The ',Puerta del Perdon,' and the ' Puerta de los Leones,' especially, are unique in their gorgeous details, and in the great beauty and lifelike expression of the figures.

The chapter library is in good order, and con-tains some very fine editions of Greek and Latin works : a bible belonging to St. Isidore ; the works of St. Gregory ; a fine illuminated bible given by St. Louis ; a missal of Charles V. ; a fine Talmud and Koran ; and some very interesting MSS. In the ante-room are some good pictures.

The palace of the archbishop is exactly opposite the west front of the cathedral. No one has played a more important part in the history of his coun-try of late years than the present Archbishop of Toledo. High in the favour and counsels of the queen, he at one time determined, for political reasons, to leave Spain and settle himself in Italy, . but was recalled by the voice of both queen and people, and remains, beloved and honoured by all; and although upwards of eighty years of age, and rather deaf, is still a perfect lion of intellec-

tual and physical strength. He received our
travellers most kindly, and in a fatherly manner
invited them to breakfast, and afterwards to be
present at a private confirmation in the little
chapel of his palace, at which ceremony they
gladly assisted. He afterwards sent his secretary,
a most clever and agreeable person, who spoke
Italian with fluency, to show the ladies the convent
of Sta. Teresa, situated in the lower part of the
town. This convent was started, like all the rest
of the saint's foundations, amidst discouragements
and difficulties of all kinds. The house which had
been promised her before her arrival was refused
through the intrigues of a relative of the donor ;
then the vicar-general withdrew his license ; and
St. Theresa began to fear that she would have to
leave Toledo without accomplishing her object.
Through the intervention of a poor man, however,
she at last heard of a tiny lodging where she and
her sisters could be received. It was a very humble
place, and there was but one room in it which
could be turned into a chapel; but that was duly
prepared for mass, and dedicated to St. Joseph.
Poor and meagre as the sanctuary was, it struck
a little child who was passing by, by its bright
and cared-for appearance, and she exclaimed :
' Blessed be God ! how beautiful and clean it

looks !' St. Theresa said directly to her sisters : 'I account myself well repaid for all the troubles which have attended this foundation by that little angel's one 'Glory to God.'

Afterwards, all difficulties were smoothed ; a larger house was built ; and the poor Carmelites, from being despised and rejected by all, and in want of the commonest necessaries of life, were overwhelmed with supplies of all kinds, so that one of them, in sorrow, exclaimed to St. Theresa: 'What are we to do, Mother ? for now it seems that we are no longer poor !'

It was this very house which our travellers now visited, and a far cheerier and brighter one it is than that of Seville. It contains twenty-four sisters : among their treasures are the MS. copy of St. Theresa's 'Way of Perfection,' corrected by the saint herself, and with a short preface written in her own hand ; a quantity of her autograph letters ; a long letter from sister Ann of St. Bartholomew ; St. Theresa's seal, of which the ladies were given an impression ; the habit she had worn in the house, &c., &c. But the most curious thing was the picture, painted by desire of the saint, of the death of one of the community. We will tell the story in her own words : 'One of our sisters fell dangerously ill, and I went to pray for her before the

Blessed Sacrament, beseeching our Lord to give her a happy death. I then came back to her cell to stay with her, and on my entrance distinctly saw a figure like the representations of our Lord, at the bed's head, with His arms outspread as if protecting her, and He said to me : " Be assured that in like manner I will protect all the nuns who shall die in these monasteries, so that they shall not fear any temptation at the hour of death." A short time after, I spoke to her, when she said to me : " Mother, what great things I am about to see ! " and with these words she expired, like an angel.' St. Theresa had this subject represented in a fresco, which is still on the wall of the cell. Here also she completed the narrative of her life, now in the Escurial, by command of Padre Ibañez, and here is her breviary, with the words (which we will give in English) written by herself on the fly-leaf :—

Let nothing disturb thee ;
Let nothing affright thee;
All passeth away ;
   God only shall stay.
Patience wins all.
Who hath God needeth nothing,
   For God is his All.

Leaving this interesting convent, our travellers proceeded to San Juan de los Reyes, so called

because built by Ferdinand and Isabella, and dedicated to St. John.   It was a magnificent Gothic
building ; but the only thing in the church spared
by the French are two exquisite 'palcos' or balconies overlooking the high altar, in the finest Gothic carving, from whence Ferdinand and Isabella
used to hear mass : their cyphers are beautifully
wrought in stone underneath.   Outside this church
hang the chains which were taken off the Christian prisoners when they were released from the
Moors.   Adjoining is the convent, now deserted,
and the palace of Cardinal Ximenes, of which the
staircase and one long low room alone remain.
But the gem of the whole are the cloisters.   Never
was anything half so beautiful or so delicate as
the Moorish tracery and exquisite patterns of
grape-vine, thistle, and acanthus, carved round
each quaint-shaped arch and window and doorway.   Festoons of real passion flowers, in full
bloom, hung over the arches from the 'patio' in
the centre, in which a few fine cypresses and pome-
granates were also growing, the dark foliage
standing out against the bright blue sky overhead,
and beautifully contrasting with the delicate white
marble tracery of this exquisite double cloister.
It is a place where an artist might revel for a
month.

Their guide then took them to see the synagogues, now converted into Christian churches, but originally mosques. Exquisite Saracenic carvings remain on the walls and roofs, with fine old Moorish capitals to the pillars, of their favourite pine-apple pattern, and beautiful coloured 'azulejos' (tiles) on the floors and seats. Several of the private houses which they afterwards visited at Toledo might literally have been taken up at Damascus and set down in this quaint old Spanish town, so identical are they in design, in decorations, and in general character. The nails on the doors are specially quaint, mostly of the shape of big mushrooms, and the knockers are also wonderful. Could the fashion once in vogue among 'fast' men in England, of wrenching such articles from the doors, be introduced into Spain, what art treasures one could get!—but scarcely anything of the sort is to be bought in Toledo. After trying in vain to swallow some of the food prepared for them at the 'fonda,' in which it was hard to say whether garlic or rancid oil most predominated, our travellers toiled again in the burning sun up the steep hill leading to the Alcazar, the ancient palace, now a ruin, but still retaining its fine old staircase and court-yard with very ancient Roman pillars. From hence there is a beautiful view of

the town, of the Tagus flowing round it, and
of the picturesque one-arched bridge which spans
the river in the approach from Madrid, with the
ruins of the older Roman bridge and forts below.
The Tagus here rushes down a rapid with a fine
fall, looking like a salmon-leap, where there ought
to be first-rate pools and beautiful fishing; and
then flows swiftly and silently along through
a grand gorge of rocks to the left.   By the river-
side was the Turkish water-wheel, or ' sakeel,'
worked by mules.   The whole thing was thoroughly Eastern ; and the red, barren, arid look of
the rocks and of the whole surrounding country
reminded one more of Syria than of anything
European.   Our travellers were leaning over the
parapet of the little terrace-garden, looking on this
glorious view, when a group of women who were
sitting in the sun near the palace gates called to
their guide, and asked if the lady of the party were
an Englishwoman, ' as she walked so fast.'   The
guide replied in the affirmative.   One of them answered, ' O! qué peccado ! (what a pity !)   I liked
her face, and *yet she is an infidel.'*   The guide indignantly pointed to a little crucifix which hung
on a rosary by the lady's side, at which the speaker,
springing from her seat, impulsively kissed both
the cross and the lady.   This is only a speci-

men of the faith of these people, who cannot understand anything Christian that is not Catholic, and confound all Protestants with Jews or Moors.*

Going down the hill, stopping only for a few moments at a curiosity shop—where, however, nothing really old could be obtained—they came to the Church of La Cruz, built on the site of the martyrdom of St. Leocadia. It is now turned

---

* In one of Fernan Caballero's novels this feeling is amusingly described. An Andalusian is telling the story of a countryman of his who had travelled in the North—'"where the earth is covered with so thick a mantle of snow that sometimes people were buried under it." "María Santísima!" said Maria, trembling. "But they are quiet people, and do not use the stiletto." "God bless them!" exclaimed Maria. "In that land there are no olives, and they eat black bread." "A bad land for me," observed Ana, "for I must have the best bread, if I can't have anything else." "What *gazpachos* could they make without olive-oil, and with black bread?" cried Maria, hor-r'fied. "They don't eat 'gazpachos.'" "What *do* they eat then?" "Potatoes and milk." "Bien provecho y salud para el pecho!" (Much good may it do them!) "But the worst is this, Maria, that in all that land there are no monks or nuns." "What do you say, son?" said she. "What you hear. There are few churches, and these look like unfurnished hospitals, without chapels, altars, or santissimo." "Jesu Maria!" exclaimed all but Maria, who, with terror, had become like a statue. Then, after a while, she crossed her hands with joyful fervour, and exclaimed: "Ah! my son! Ah! my white bread! My church, my most Blessed Virgin, my land, my faith, my 'Dios Sacramentado!' A thousand times happier I, who was born here, and by grace Divine will die here. Thanks be to God, you did not stay in that land, my son! A land of heretics! how horrible!!"'

into a military college ; but the magnificent Gothic portal and façade remain. The streets are as narrow and dirty in this part of the town as in the filthiest Eastern city ; but at every turn there is a beautiful doorway, as at Cairo, through which you peep into a cool ' patio,' with its usual fountain and orange-trees ; while a double cloister runs round the quadrangle, and generally a picturesque side staircase, with a beautifully carved balustrade, leading up to the cloisters above, with their delicate tracery and varied arches. The beauty of the towers and ' campanile ' is also very striking. They are generally thoroughly Roman in their character, being built of that narrow brick (or rather tile) so common for the purpose in Italy, but with the horse-shoe arch : that of S. Romano is the most perfect. There is also a lovely little mosque, with a well in the courtyard near the entrance, which has now been converted into a church under the title of ' Sta. Cruz de la Luz,' with a wonderful intersection of horse-shoe arches, like a miniature of the cathedral at Cordova. Toledo certainly does not lack churches or convents ; but those who served and prayed in them, where are they ? The terrible want of instruction for the people, caused by the closing of all the male religious houses, which

Church of La Cruz, Toledo.

were the centre of all missionary work, is felt throughout Spain ; but nowhere more than in this grand old town, which is absolutely *dead.* The children are neglected, the poor without a friend, the widow and orphan are desolate, and all seek in vain for a helper or a guide.

On the opposite side of the Tagus, and not far from the railway station, are the ruins of a curious old château, to which a legend is attached, so characteristic of the tone of thought of the people that it is given verbatim here.* ' The owner had been a bad and tyrannical man, hard and unjust to his people, selfish in his vices as in his pleasures ; the only redeeming point about him was his great love for his wife, a pious, gentle, loving woman, who spent her days and nights in deploring the orgies of her husband, and praying for God's mercy on his crimes. One winter's night, in the midst of a terrible tempest, a knocking was heard at the castle door, and presently a servant came in and told his mistress that two monks, half dead with cold and hunger, and drenched by the pitiless storm, had lost their way, and were begging for a night's lodging in the castle. The poor lady did not know what to do, for her hus-

* This legend has been translated by Fernan Caballero, in her ' Fleurs des Champs.'

band hated the monks, and swore that none should ever cross his threshold. "The count will know nothing about it, my lady," said the old servant, who guessed the reason of her hesitation; "I will conceal them somewhere in the stable, and they will depart at break of day." The lady gave a joyful assent to the servant's proposal, and the monks were admitted. Scarcely, however, had they entered, when the sound of a huntsman's horn, the tramping of horses, and the barking of dogs, announced the return of the master. The sport had been good ; and when he had changed his soiled and dripping clothes, and found himself, with his pretty wife seated opposite him, by a blazing fire, and with a well-covered table, his good humour made him almost tender towards her. "What is the matter ?" he exclaimed, when he saw her sad and downcast face. "Were you frightened at the storm ?—yet you see I am come home safe and sound." She did not answer. "Tell me what vexes you ; I insist upon it," he continued ; "and it shall not be my fault if I do not brighten that little face I love so well !" Thus encouraged, the lady replied : "I am sad, because, while we are enjoying every luxury and comfort here, others whom I know, even under this very roof, are perishing with cold and hunger."

"But who are they?" exclaimed the count, with
some impatience. "Two poor monks," answered
the lady bravely, "who came here for shelter, and
have been put in the stable without food or firing."
The count frowned. "Monks! Have I not told
you fifty times I would never have those idle
pestilent fellows in my house?" He rang the bell.
"For God's sake do not turn them out such a
night as this!" exclaimed the countess. "Don't
be afraid, I will keep my word," replied her
husband; and so saying, he desired the servant
to bring them directly into the dining-room.
They appeared; and the venerable, saint-like appearance of the elder of the two priests checked
the raillery on the lips of the count. He made
them sit down at his table; but the religious,
faithful to his mission, would not eat till he had
spoken some of God's words to his host. After
supper, to his wife's joy and surprise, the count
conducted the monks himself to the rooms he
had prepared for them, which were the best in
the house; but they refused to sleep on anything
but straw. The count then himself went and
fetched a truss of hay, and laid it on the floor.
Then suddenly breaking silence, he exclaimed:
"Father, I would return as a prodigal son to my
Father's house; but I feel as if it were impossible

that He should forgive sins like mine." "Were your sins as numberless as the grains of sand on the sea-shore," replied the missionary, "faithful repentance, through the blood of Christ, would wash them out. Therefore it is that the hardened sinner will have no excuse in the last day." Seized with sudden compunction, the count fell on his knees, and made a full confession of his whole life, his tears falling on the straw he had brought. A few hours later the missionary, in a dream, saw himself, as it were, carried before the tribunal of the Great Judge. In the scales of eternal justice a soul was to be weighed : it was that of the count. Satan, triumphant, placed in the scales the countless sins of his past life : the good angels veiled their faces in sorrow, and pity, and shame. Then came up his guardian angel, that spirit so patient and so watchful, so beautiful and so good, who brings tears to our eyes and repentance to our hearts, alms to our hands and prayers to our lips. He brought but a few bits of straw, wet with tears, and placed them in the opposite scale. Strange ! *they weighed down all the rest.* The soul was saved. The next morning, the monk, on waking, found the castle in confusion and sorrow. He enquired the reason : its master had died in the night.'

CHAPTER X.

ZARAGOZA AND SEGOVIA.

THE following morning found our travellers again in Madrid, and one of them accompanied the sisters of charity to a beautiful fête at San Juan de Alarçon, a convent of nuns. The rest of the day was spent in the museum; and at half-past eight in the evening they started again by train for Zaragoza, which they reached at six in the morning. One of the great annoyances of Spanish travelling is, that the only good and quick trains go at night; and it is the same with the diligences. In very hot weather it may be pleasant; but in winter and in rain it is a very wretched proceeding to spend half your night in an uncomfortable carriage, and the other half waiting, perhaps for hours, at some miserable wayside station. After breakfasting in an hotel where nothing was either eatable or drinkable, our party started for the two cathedrals. The one called the 'Seu' is a fine gloomy old Gothic building, with a magnificent 'retablo,' in very fine carving, over the high altar, and what the people call a 'media naranja' (or half-orange) dome, which is rather like the clerestory lantern of Burgos. In the sacristy was a beautiful ostensorium, with an emerald and pearl cross, a magnificent silver tabernacle of cinque-cento work, another ostensorium encrusted with diamonds, a nacre 'nef,' and some fine heads of saints, in silver, with enamel collars. But at the sister cathedral, where is the famous *Virgen del Pilar*, the treasury is quite priceless. The most exquisite reliquaries in pearls, precious stones, and enamel; magnificent necklaces; ear-rings with gigantic pearls; coronets of diamonds; lockets; pictures set in precious stones; everything which is most valuable and beautiful, has been lavished on this shrine. In the outside sacristy is also an exquisite chalice, in gold and enamel, of the fifteenth century; and a very fine picture, said to be by Correggio, of the 'Ecce Homo.' The shrine of the Miraculous Virgin is thronged with worshippers, day and night; but no woman is allowed to penetrate beyond the railing, so that she is very imperfectly seen. It is a *black* figure, which is always the favourite way of representing the Blessed Virgin in Spain: the pillar is of the purest alabaster. There is some fine 'azulejo' work in the sacristy; but the cathedral itself is ugly, and is being restored in a bad style. Our party left it rather with relief, and wandered down to the fine old bridge over the Ebro, which is here a broad and rapid stream, and amused themselves by watching the boats shooting through the piers—an operation of some danger, owing to the rapidity of the current. There is a beautiful leaning tower of old Moorish and Roman brickwork, in a side street, but which you are not allowed to ascend without a special order from the prefect. The Lonja, or Exchange, is also well worth seeing, from its beautiful deep overhanging roof. This is, in fact, the characteristic of all the old houses in Zaragoza, which is a quaint old town formed of a succession of narrow, tortuous streets, with curious old roofs, 'patios,' columns, and staircases. After having some luncheon, which was more eatable than the breakfast, our travellers took a drive outside the town, and had a beautiful view of the lower spur of the Pyrenees on the one hand, and of the towers, bridges, and minarets of the city on the other. Then they went to the public gardens, laid out by Pignatelli, the maker of the canal, which are the resort of all the people on fête-days : they were very gay, and full of beautiful flowers. From thence they drove

P

to the castle, or ' Aljaferia,' where there is a very curious moresque chapel still existing, though sadly in ruins. Above are the rooms occupied by Ferdinand and Isabella, and the apartment where St. Elizabeth of Portugal was born, with the font where she was baptized. The Hall of the Ambassadors is very handsome, with a glorious moresque roof, and a gallery round. The castle is now turned into a barrack; but the officers, who, with true Spanish courtesy, had accompanied the priest who was showing the rooms to our travellers, *had never seen them before themselves.* How long they had been quartered there none of our party had the courage to ask ! But this is a specimen of the very little interest which appears to be taken by the Spaniards in the antiquities or art treasures of their country. Not one of them was ever to be seen in the matchless gallery of Madrid. Coming home, they visited San Pablo, a curious and beautiful subterranean church, into which you descend by a flight of steps. A service was going on, and an eloquent sermon, so that it was impossible to see the pictures well; but they appeared to be above the average. This church has a glorious tower in old Roman brickwork. The palace of the Infanta has been converted into a school. It is the most perfect spe-

cimen of the Renaissance style of Gothic architecture, with beautiful arches, columns, staircase,
and fretted roof. Exhausted with their sight-
seeing, our travellers went back to their inn;
agreeably surprised, however, at the vestiges of
ancient beauty still left in Zaragoza, after the
frightful sieges and sacking to which the city has
twice been subjected.

In the evening, the Canon de V——, who
had been their kind cicerone at the cathedral in
the absence of the bishop, came to pay them a
visit, and gave them a very interesting account
of the people, and a great deal of information
about the convents and religious houses in the
place, especially that of the Ursulines, who have
a very large educational establishment in the
town. He has lately written a very interesting
account of the foundress of this order.

The return to Madrid was necessarily accomplished again by night; and jaded and tired as
they were the following day, our party had not the
courage for any fresh expedition. One only visit
was paid, which will ever remain in the memory of
the lady who had the privilege. It was to Monsignor Claret, the confessor of the queen and Archbishop of Cuba, a man as remarkable for his great
personal holiness and ascetic life as for the un-

just accusations of which he is continually the
object.   On one occasion, these unfavourable re-
ports having reached his ears, and being only
anxious to retire into the obscurity which his
humility makes him love so well, he went to
Rome to implore for a release from his present
post ; but it was refused him.   Returning through
France, he happened to travel with certain gentlemen, residents in Madrid, but unknown to
him, as he was to them, who began to speak
of all the evils, real or imaginary, which reigned
in the Spanish Court, the whole of which they
unhesitatingly attributed to Monsignor Claret,
very much in the spirit of the old ballad against
Sir Robert Peel :—

> Who filled the butchers' shops with big blue flies ?

He listened without a word, never attempting
either excuse or justification, or betraying his
identity.   Struck with his saint-like manner and
appearance, and likewise very much charmed
with his conversation during their couple of
days' journey together, the strangers begged, at
parting, to know his name, expressing an earnest hope of an increased acquaintance at Madrid.
He gave them his card with a smile !   Let us
hope they will be less hasty and more charitable

in their judgments for the future. Monsignor Claret's room in Madrid is a fair type of himself. Simple even to severity in its fittings, with no furniture but his books, and some photographs of the queen and her children, it contains one only priceless object, and that is a wooden crucifix, of the very finest Spanish workmanship, which attracted at once the attention of his visitor. 'Yes, it is very beautiful,' he replied, in answer to her words of admiration ; ' and I like it because it expresses so wonderfully *victory over suffering.* Crucifixes generally represent only the painful and human, not the triumphant and Divine view of the Redemption. Here, He is truly Victor over death and hell.'

Contrary to the generally received idea, he never meddles in politics, and occupies himself entirely in devotional and literary works. One of his books, ' Camino recto y seguro para llegar al Cielo,' would rank with Thomas à Kempis's ' Imitation ' in suggestive and practical devotion. He keeps a perpetual fast ; and when compelled by his position to dine at the palace, still keeps to his meagre fare of ' garbanzos,' or the like. He has a great gift of preaching ; and when he accompanies the queen in any of her royal progresses, is generally met at each town when they

arrive by earnest petitions to preach, which he
does instantly, without rest or apparent prepara-
tion, sometimes delivering four or five sermons
in one day. In truth, he is always ' prepared,' by
a hidden life of perpetual prayer and realisation
of the Unseen.

After taking leave of him and the Nunzio, and
of the many other kind friends who had made
their stay at Madrid so pleasant, our travellers
started at eight o'clock in the evening for Villa
Alba, where they were to take the diligence for
Segovia. The night was clear and beautiful, and
the scenery through which they passed was finer
than any they had seen in Spain. At dawn they
came almost suddenly on this most quaint and
picturesque of cities, standing on a rocky knoll
more than 3,000 feet above the sea, encircled
by a rapid river, and with the most magnificent aqueduct, built by Trajan to convey the
pure water of the river Frio from the neighbouring sierra to the town. This aqueduct com-
mences with single arches, which rise higher as
the dip of the ground deepens, until they become double. The centre ones are 102 feet high,
and the whole is built of massive blocks of
granite, without cement or mortar. A succession of picturesque towers and ancient walls

remain to mark the boundaries of the old Roman city.

The diligence unceremoniously turned our travellers out into the street at the bottom of the town, and left them to find their way as best they could to the little 'fonda' in the square above. It was very clean and tidy, with the box-beds opening out of the sitting-rooms, which are universal in the old-fashioned inns of Spain, and always remind one of a Highland bothie. The daughter of the house showed off her white linen with great pride, and was rather affronted because two of the party preferred going to church to trying her sheets, stoutly declaring that 'no one was yet awake, and no mass could yet be obtained.' However, on leaving her, and gently pushing open one of the low side-doors of the cathedral close by, the ladies found that the five o'clock services had begun at most of the altars, with a very fair sprinkling of peasants at each. The circular triple apse at the east end of this cathedral, from the warm colour of the stone, and the beauty of its flying buttresses and Gothic pinnacles, is deservedly reckoned one of the finest in Spain. The tower also is beautiful; and the view from the cupola over the city, the fertile valleys beneath, and the snow-tipped mountains beyond, is quite unrivalled. The interior has been a good deal spoiled by modern innovations, but still contains some glorious painted glass, a very fine 'retablo' by Juni of the 'Deposition from the Cross,' and some curious monuments, especially one of the Infanta Don Pedro, son of Henry II., who was killed by being let fall from the window of the Alcazar by his nurse. The Gothic cloisters are also worth seeing. After service, as it was still very early, the two ladies wandered about this beautiful quaint old town, in which every house is a study for a painter, and found themselves at last at the Alameda, a public promenade on the ramparts, shaded by fine acacias, and the approach to which, on the cathedral side, is through a beautiful Moorish horse-shoe arched gateway. From thence some stone steps led them up to a most curious old Norman church, with an open cloister running round it, with beautiful circular arches and dog-toothed mouldings; opposite is a kind of Hôtel de Ville, with a fine gateway, cloistered 'patio,' and staircase carved 'à jour.' In a narrow street, a little lower down, is the exquisite Gothic façade of the Casa de Segovia, and turning to the left is another curious and beautiful church, La Vera Cruz, built by the Templars, and with a little chapel in it on the exact model of that of the Holy Sepulchre at Jerusalem. The zigzag and billet dog-tooth mouldings round the windows and doorways are very fine. A little higher up is the Parral, a deserted convent, with a beautiful church, richly carved portal and choir, fine monuments, cloisters, and gardens : the latter had such a reputation that they gave rise to the saying, ' Las huertas del Parral, paraiso terrenal.' Fairly tired out with sight-seeing before break-fast, the ladies climbed up again to the Plaza de la Constitucion, which was like the square of an old German town, having endlessly varied and co-loured houses with high roofs ; and were glad to find the rest of the party awake at last, and sitting round a table with the invariably good chocolate and white bread of the country. The meal over, one of the ladies started off, with a little boy as her guide, to present her letters of introduction to the bishop, who lived in a picturesque old palace in the Plaza of San Esteban, the fine church oppo-site, with its beautiful tower, Saxon arches, and open cloister, being dedicated to that saint. He re-ceived his visitor with great good-nature, and in-stantly countersigned the Nunzio's order for her to visit the Carmelite convent of Sta. Teresa, sending his vicar-general to accompany her. This house is the original one purchased for the saint, in 1574, by Doña Ana de Ximenes, who was the first lady to receive the habit in Segovia. It is dedicated to St. Joseph, and the first mass was said in it by St. John of the Cross. The nuns maintain the reformed rule in all its austerity. They showed their visitor the saint's cell, now converted into an oratory, and also the room of St. John of the Cross, whose convent is in the valley below, just outside the walls of the town. There his body rests—that body still uncorrupted, of one of whom it has been truly said, that he was a ' cherub in wisdom and a seraph in love.' On the door of his cell is his favourite sentence :—

Pati et contemni pro Te !

This convent is rich both in his letters and in those of St. Theresa. Here it was that the saint received the news of the death of her favourite brother, Laurence de Cepeda. She was quietly at work during recreation when he appeared to her ; the saint, without uttering a word, put down her work and hastened to the choir to commend the departing spirit to our Lord. She had no sooner knelt before the Blessed Sacrament than an expression of intense peace and joy came over her face. Her sisters asked her the reason, and she told them that our Lord had then revealed to her the assurance that her brother was in heaven. His sudden death occurred at the very moment when he had appeared to her in the recreation room. Over the door of her oratory are the words : ' Seek the cross ; ' ' Desire the cross ; ' and a little farther on, ' Let us teach more by works than by words.' After spending two or three hours with the sisters, the English lady was compelled reluctantly to leave them and return to her party, who were waiting for her to go with them to the Alcazar.

This palace, originally Moorish, was rebuilt by Henry IV. in the fifteenth century. It was the favourite residence of Isabella of Castile, and from thence, on the occasion of a revolution, she rode out alone, and ' by her sweetness of countenance more than by her majesty,' as the old chronicle says, ' won over the people to return to their allegiance.' Our King Charles I. lodged here also, and is recorded to have supped on certain ' troutes of extraordinary greatness,' doubtless from the beautiful stream below. At the time of the French invasion the Alcazar was turned into a military college, and these wretched students, in a freak of boyish folly, set fire to a portion of one of the rooms two years ago. The fire spread ; and all that is now left of this matchless palace is a ruined

shell, the façade, the beautiful Moorish towers and
battlements, one or two sculptured arabesque ceilings, and the portcullised gateway, each and all
testifying to its former greatness and splendour.
Its position, perched on a steep plateau forming
the western extremity of the town, is quite magnificent, and the views from the windows are glorious.
Our travellers stayed a long time sitting under
the shade of the orange-trees in the battlemented
court below, enjoying the glorious panorama at
their feet, and watching the setting sun as it lit up
the tips of the snowy sierra which forms the background of this grand landscape; while the beautiful
river Eresma flowed swiftly round the old walls,
its banks occupied at that moment by groups of
washerwomen in their bright picturesque dresses,
singing in parts the national songs of their country.   In the valley below were scattered home-
steads and convents, and a group of cypresses
marking the spot where, according to the legend,
Maria del Salto alighted.   This girl was a Jewess
by birth, but secretly a Christian; and having
thereby excited the anger and suspicions of her
family, was accused by them of adultery, and
condemned, according to the barbarous practice
of those times, to be thrown from the top of the
Alcazar rock.   By her faith she was miraculously

preserved from injury, and reached the ground in safety; a church was built on the spot, of which the 'retablo' tells the tale.

Segovia is famous for its flocks, and for the beauty of its wool : the water of the Eresma is supposed to be admirable for washing and shearing.

Our travellers now began to think of pursuing their journey to Avila; but that was not so easy. The diligence which had brought them, flatly refused to convey them back till the following night, except at a price so exorbitant that it was impossible to give it. And here, as everywhere else in Spain, you have no redress. There are no carriages whatever for hire, except in the two or three large capitals, like Madrid and Seville ; and even should carriages be found, there are no horses or mules to draw them—or, at any rate, none that they choose to let out for the purpose. Such as they are, they are always reserved for the diligence ; and if the latter should happen to be full, the unhappy passengers may wait for days at a wayside 'posada' until their turn comes. Therefore, it is absolutely necessary in Spain to write and make the contract for places beforehand : and to be hard-hearted when the time comes ,as it almost invariably happens that you leave behind certain luckless travellers who have

not adopted a similar precaution ; and the struggle for seats, and consequent overcrowding of the
carriages, are renewed at every station. Making
a virtue of necessity, our travellers at last made
up their minds to another miserable diligence
night out of bed—the fatigue of which must be
felt to be thoroughly sympathised with—and
spent the intervening hours of the evening in
dining, and then going to a religious play, which
they had seen advertised in the morning, and
which was a very curious exhibition of popular taste and religious feeling.   The little theatre
was really very clean and tidy, and there was
nothing approaching to irreverence in the representations given.   A similar scene in a very
different place recurred to the memory of one of
the party, as having been witnessed by her in
Paris, some years ago, when on a certain occasion she accompanied a somewhat stiff, puritanical
old lady to the opera.   A ballet was given as an
entr'acte, in which the scenery was taken from
the Book of Genesis, and Noah and his sons
appeared just coming out of the Ark.   This was
too much for the good lady : ' If Noah either
dances or sings,' she exclaimed, ' I'll leave the
house ! '   The poor Segovians, trained in a different school, saw nothing incongruous in the repre-

sentation of the shepherds, and the wise men, and the cave of Bethlehem : and only one comical incident occurred, when, on a child in the pit setting up a squeal, there was a universal cry of *Where's Herod?* At ten o'clock they left their play, with its quiet and respectable little audience, and once more found themselves tightly stowed in their diligence prison for the night. The moon, however, was bright and beautiful, and enabled them to see the royal hunting-box and woods, and the rest of the fine scenery through which they passed, so that the journey was far less intolerable than usual, as is often the case when a thing has been much dreaded beforehand. At four o'clock in the morning they were turned out, shivering with cold, at a wayside station, where they were to take the train to Avila; but were then told, to their dismay, by a sleepy porter that the six o'clock train had been taken off, and that there would be none till ten the next morning, so that all hopes of arriving at Avila in time for church (and this was Sunday) were at an end. The station had no waiting-room, only a kind of corridor with two hard benches. Establishing the children on these for the moment with plaids and shawls, one of the party went off to some cottages at a little distance off, and asked in one of them if there were no means of getting a bedroom and some chocolate? A very civil woman got up and volunteered both; so the tired ones of the party were able to lie down for a few hours' rest in two wonderfully clean little rooms, while their breakfast was preparing. The question now arose for the others : ' Was there no church anywhere near?' It was answered by the people of the place in the negative. 'The station was new; the cottages had been run up for the accommodation of the porters and people engaged on the line ; there was no village within a league or two.' Determined, however, not to be baffled, one of the party enquired of another man, who was sleepily driving his bullocks into a neighbouring field, and he replied 'that over the mountains to the left there was a village and a curé; but that it was a long way off, and that he only went on great "festas." ' It was now quite light ; the lady was strong and well; and so she determined to make the attempt to find the church. Following the track pointed out to her by her informant, she came to a wild and beautiful mountain path, intersected by bright rushing streams, crossed by stepping-stones, the ground perfectly carpeted with wild narcissus and other spring flowers. Here and there she met a peasant

tending his flock of goats, and always the courteous greeting of ' Vaya Usted con Dios !' or ' Dios
guarde á Usted !' as heartily given as returned.
At last, on rounding a corner of the mountain,
she came on a beautiful view, with the Escurial in
the distance to the left; and to the right, embe-
somed, as it were, in a little nest among the hills,
a picturesque village, with its church-tower and
rushing stream and flowering fruit-trees, towards
which the path evidently led. This sight gave
her fresh courage ; for the night journey and long
walk, undertaken fasting, had nearly spent her
strength.   Descending the hill rapidly, she reached
the village green just as the clock was striking
six, and found a group of peasants, both men and
women, sitting on the steps of the picturesque
stone cross in the centre, opposite the church,
waiting for the curé to come out of his neat little
house close by to say the first mass.   The arrival
of the lady caused some astonishment ; but, with
the inborn courtesy of the people, one after the
other rose and came forward, not only to greet
her, but to offer her chocolate and bread.   She
explained that she had come for communion, and
would go into the church.   The old white-haired
clerk ran into the house to hasten the curé, and
soon a kind and venerable old man made his

Q

appearance, and asked her if she wished to see him first in the confessional. He could scarcely believe she had been in Segovia only the night before! Finding that she was hurried to return and catch the train, he instantly gave her both mass and communion, and then sent his housekeeper to invite her to breakfast, as did one after the other of the villagers. Escaping from their hospitality with some difficulty, on the plea of the shortness of the time and the length of the way back, the English lady accepted a little loaf, for which no sort of payment would be heard of, and walked with a light heart back to the station, feeling how close is the religious tie which binds Catholics together as one family, and how beautiful is the hearty, simple hospitality of the Spanish people when untainted by contact with modern innovations and so-called progress. There was no occasion when this natural, high-bred courtesy was not shown during the four months that our travellers spent in this country; and those who, like the author of 'Over the Pyrenees into Spain,' find fault on every occasion with the manners of the people, must either have been ignorant of their language and customs, or, having no sympathy with their faith, have wounded their susceptibilities, and to a certain degree justified the rudeness of which they pretend to have been the victims.

West Door of Cathedral of Avila.

CHAPTER XI.

AVILA AND ALVA.

AFTER a clean and plentiful breakfast in the cottage, our party started by train for Avila, where they arrived at one o'clock ; and having washed and dressed, found themselves at vespers at the cathedral, which is a beautiful Gothic build-ing, begun in 1107, with a glorious western façade, . a very fine circular apse at the east end, grand monuments, and magnificent painted glass. The 'retablo' over the high altar is in better taste than almost any in Spain, and contains some beauti-fully carved subjects, especially one of the 'An-nunciation.' Both this cathedral and the clois-ters are built of a peculiar shaded red and white granite, unlike any other, but which gives rather the effect of the cathedral of Sienna. After vespers. some of the party went to the arch-bishop's, who was absent on a confirmation tour, but had left orders that they should be received, boarded, and lodged at his palace, and had desired his vicar-general to do the honours in his absence. This hospitality our party considered themselves too numerous to accept, and they had already found very tolerable accommodation in a little 'fonda' opposite the cathedral; but they gladly accepted the offer of his kind and courteous secretary to act as their escort, especially for the inspection of St. Theresa's house and convent on the following day.

Avila is a noble specimen of an old Castilian fortified city, teeming with curious Gothic monuments and inscriptions of the thirteenth century, which, unfortunately, no one seems to care for or to be able to explain. Fragments of these are worked into every house : at every turn are quaint old basilicas with circular apses, beautiful doorways and dog-tooth mouldings. Of these, the finest is that of S. Vincente, in a ' plaza ' on the way leading to the railway station. It contains the body of St. Vincent, who suffered in the Decian persecution. His monument, on raised twisted pillars, is in the centre of the church. There is a subterranean crypt, which also contains the bodies of martyrs and several fine monuments. The tower, cloisters, and portico, with clustered columns, are beautiful ; and from the cloister there is a magnificent view over the rich 'vega'

beneath, and of the unique east end of the cathedral built into the city wall.

This is almost the only place our travellers
had yet seen in Spain where the women wore the
old national costume. In Granada, Cordova, and
Seville, the men retain their picturesque dresses;
but their wives rarely do so. Here the women
are all dressed in bright yellow canary-coloured
stuff petticoats, with red cloth 'appliquéed' in
patterns, on the skirt, green or red bodices,
strings of pearls, and hair in circular rolls on the
side of the head, with pins across each. From
the bridge, the view of the river, of the towers,
(of which there are eighty-eight), and of the
grand old crenellated walls which encircle the
town, is very fine. The following morning, after
high mass at the cathedral, one of the party
started with the vicar-general to see the house in
which St. Theresa was born. On their way they
passed by the beautiful palace of the Medina
Cœli, which has the arms of the family (thirteen
balls) over the door, and four of those curious
granite rhinoceros, or 'toros,' as the people call
them, found here and there in Spain, the origin
of which is so disputed by the learned. There is
also a curious inscription on a bas-relief over the
principal entrance, in old and quaint Spanish,

the meaning of which in English would be : 'When one door shuts, another opens,' probably alluding to some family legend now forgotten.

St. Theresa was the daughter of Alonso de Cepeda and Beatrix de Ahumada, both of noble and even royal blood, and it was in their house that our party now found themselves. It is a beautiful palace, which has passed through many phases, having become, after St. Theresa's death, a Carmelite monastery; and now, since the destruction of the religious houses in Spain, a college for boys. There is a very fine church attached to it, full of beautiful marbles and frescoes ; and leading out of this church is the room of Madame de Cepeda, in which Theresa was born. It has been converted into a chapel. Here are kept her bedstead, part of which was made into a cross ; her rosary ; her walking-stick, with a crook for the thumb; her shoes, &c., &c. Everything belonging to her, however remotely, is preserved with a veneration which it would be almost impossible to imagine out of Spain.

From thence, they went on to the convent of St. Joseph, called 'de las Madres,' being her first reformed foundation. A statue of the saint is placed over the portal. Here, on St. Bartholomew's-day, 1562, St. Theresa saw at last the

accomplishment of her prayers : here, the habit
of rough serge and the veil of coarse unbleached
linen were first given to the four sisters of the
new reform, which was afterwards to embrace so
many thousand devout and holy souls. In the
church are the tombs of her favourite brother
Lorenzo, and of the good Bishop of Avila, Alva-
rez de Mendoza, through whose powerful protection this first house was started, and who chose
to be buried in this humble little chapel sooner
than in his own beautiful cathedral, in the hope,
which was not destined to be realised, of resting
near the saint. St. Peter of Alacantara's letter
to this bishop, when pleading for permission for
the foundation, is among the treasures contained
in this convent. The superior and the sisters
received their English visitor most kindly, and
showed her everything. The saint's cell, now
converted into an oratory; her bed; her chair;
her clothes; the coffin in which her body was
placed before it was removed to Alva; her jug
and cup; her musical instruments; her leathern
girdle; her discipline; some of her blood; a
bone of her neck; her books and letters. Among
the books is a folio in two volumes of St. Gregory's 'Morales,' belonging to St. Theresa, with
her notes and marks; a book written by St.

John of the Cross, with annotations on a kind
of 'Canzone' of Ann of St. Bartholomew ; and
a MS. copy of the saint's 'Foundations.'   In
the hermitages which she founded in the garden
are some very curious pictures belonging to the
saint, and some old engravings.   One picture
was painted by her desire, in consequence of a
vision in which she saw our Lord bound to the
pillar after the scourging.   These hermitages
were constructed so that the nuns might have
less interruption in the quiet and fervency of
their prayers.   The well still remains in the
garden, of which the water was at first so bad
that they could not use it ; and then, by the simple
prayer of faith of these poor nuns, it pleased God
so to sweeten it that it has been ever since good
and sufficient for the wants of the community.
Here, after all the storms and difficulties she had
had to encounter, St. Theresa spent five years
in comparative peace and happiness.   She had
thirteen sisters in this house, all of whom were
endowed with such rare spiritual gifts, that the
saint declared 'she was ashamed to live amongst
them herself.'   Yet, even here, she had much to
suffer.   One day, as she was ascending the steps
which led to the choir, before compline, she was
suddenly thrown down, falling with such violence

that her nuns thought she was killed. They
found, however, that only her arm was broken.
According to the rough surgery of those days,
the female practitioner, who had been sent for,
went to work so violently to set the broken
limb that the bones were dislocated. Theresa
did not utter a cry, but contemplated all the
time the violence with which our Lord was
stretched on the cross, telling her sisters that she
should have been sorry to have missed this op-
portunity of suffering something with patience.
These steps are still shown, as also a picture
representing the occurrence.

From St. Joseph's the English lady went on to
the convent of the Incarnation, the house where
St. Theresa made her first profession of religion,
and in which more than twenty years of her life
were passed. A prophecy preceded her arrival. A
stranger had come to the convent a short time
before, and said, ' A saint will shortly come to dwell
in this house, whose name will be Theresa.' When
told of this prophecy, St. Theresa, then a young
and merry novice, laughingly said to a com-
panion, who also bore the name : ' Which of us
two shall be the saint ? ' This convent is in a
beautiful situation, in a fertile valley, at a little
distance from the town, with a fine church,

magnificent cloisters, and a spacious garden and
orchard, watered by a clear quick-flowing stream.
Among the treasures in this house are the veil
and dress in which she made her first religious
profession ; the wooden crucifix and the infant
Jesus which she always carried about with her
in her travels, and used for her mass in her
first foundations ; her room, chair, and pictures ;
and quantities of letters, both of St. Theresa's
and of St. John of the Cross, who was prior and
confessor of the convent.   One of the saint's
letters is countersigned by the four nuns of the
first foundation : Antonia of the Holy Ghost
Mary of the Cross, Ursula of the Saints, and Mary
of St. Joseph.   Here also is a very curious picture, painted by the saint's desire, of St. Peter
of Alacantara as he appeared to her in a vision
after his death, saying : ' My present glory,
through the mercy of Christ, is the fruit of my
penitence.'   A few years after St. Theresa had
left this house for those of her reform, that is, in
1571, she was appointed, by the provincial,
superior of this convent of the Incarnation, in
order to remedy the evils which existed in the
house.   This caused a furious storm, which was
only quelled by Theresa's wonderful prudence,
humility, and gentleness.   The day the first

chapter was held, the nuns came in a body prepared to rebel. But in the place of the prioress,
they found only a beautiful statue of the Virgin,
holding the keys of the convent, and St. Theresa,
addressing them as the most unworthy member
of the house, only craved permission to aid them
in every way in her power. As is admirably
said by the clever authoress of her 'Life,' before
alluded to : ' Those who had been accustomed
to look upon the saint as a visionary enthusiast,
were both astonished and touched by the ready
presence of mind and the minute solicitude with
which she regulated all the complicated worldly
affairs of the community, and supplied the most
trifling wants of each of its members.' The little
parlour is still shown where the saint and St.
John of the Cross were found raised from the
ground in an ecstacy while discoursing on the
love of God ; which can only be explained
by the saint's own words : 'It is certain that
when for the love of God we empty our souls
of all affection for creatures, that great God im-
mediately fills them with Himself.'

There are seventeen nuns in this house, and
their veneration for the saint seems as great as
that of her sisters of the reform.

Returning to the ' fonda,' and taking leave of

the kind vicar-general and this most interesting
old town, our travellers started at two o'clock
in the morning by diligence for Salamanca.
Of course, the diligence authorities would not
condescend to come up to the 'fonda' to fetch
the ladies, who had no alternative but to grope
their way through the streets in pitchy darkness,
amidst torrents of rain, and under cut-throat-
looking archways, until they reached the grimy,
undesirable vehicle.

The country, after leaving Avila, is hideously
flat and ugly, more like an old post-road through
parts of France or Hanover than anything they
had hitherto seen in Spain. Salamanca itself
stands on a height, the river Tormes encircling
the town, over which is thrown a very fine
Roman bridge of twenty-seven arches. The
diligence dragged them painfully up the steep
streets and over the horribly disjointed pavement to the Plaza Mayor, the largest square in
Spain, of which the façade is adorned with busts
of kings, and with a colonnaded arcade all round,
looking like Bologna. Here the bull-fights are
held; and with more humanity than at Seville,
the horses being almost invariably saved from injury. The 'posada' in the Plaza was so uninviting
that our party betook themselves to a private lodg-

ing in a side street, which had been recommended
to them at Avila. Here they found some very nice
clean rooms and the best food they had had since
leaving Madrid. After changing their crumpled
and dusty clothes (for one of the many miseries of
diligence travelling is the dust), they started off
for the cathedrals, for there are *two*, one above the
other. The one below is simple, massive, and what
we call Norman in character; the one above is
the most florid and elaborate Gothic. The carving of the portal and of the whole façade of the
west front is the most gorgeous and beautiful
thing which it is possible to conceive. One's
breath is fairly taken away by the number and
variety of the figures. Inside, its principal features are the height of the arches and the beautiful open pierced work of the galleries which
run round the cathedral. The rest has a new,
white, cold look, which did not please eyes accustomed to the solemn sober aisles of Seville.
In the sacristy are some curious pictures and
relics; among others, ' El Crucifijo de las Batallas,'
a small Byzantine bronze crucifix which the Cid
always carried before him in battle, and some
very interesting letters of St. Theresa's.

Nearly opposite the cathedral is the far-famed
University, of which the magnificent façade is

alone worth a journey to Salamanca to see. It is in the richest period of Ferdinand and Isabella, whose badges are worked into the arabesque lace-like scrolls, together with the inscription in Greek : ' The fear of the Lord is the beginning of wisdom.' Equally elaborate is the carving of the façade of San Esteban, in a ' plaza ' a little below the cathedral. The beautiful creamy colour of the stone adds immensely to the effect of all this work. But the French destroyed and desecrated every religious building in Salamanca : only ruined cloisters, bare refectories, and mutilated doorways remain to testify to past beauties.

From the cathedral our travellers went up the steep hill to the Irish College, having a letter from the English minister at Madrid to the principal ; but he was ill and unable to see them. His students, however, received them with hearty expressions of welcome, and offered to be their cicerones during their stay in Salamanca. It was so curious to hear a very decided Irish brogue in the ' patio ' of a Spanish convent. But their numbers are few ; and the University itself has dwindled down to 400 or 500 students instead of the 17,000 talked of in the sixteenth century. Cardinal Ximenes was once tutor in a

Palace. Guadalajara.

college here; and Cervantes lived for a long time in a house still pointed out as his in the Calle de los Moros. The palaces in Salamanca are very beautiful, especially the Casa de las Conchas, so called from the pecten shells projecting out of each stone; the Casa de las Salinas, with its overhanging roof and gallery and richly ornamented windows; and the Palacio del Conde de Monterey, with its turrets and an upper gallery of arcaded windows, which look like the rich lace fringe of the solid building below. After lionising the whole morning, one of the party went to call on the bishop, a man universally esteemed and beloved in Salamanca, who received his visitor with fatherly kindness, and at once volunteered to walk with her and show her the different conventual establishments, which she had obtained Papal permission to see. The lady soon found, however, that walking with the bishop, though a great honour, was a matter of some difficulty. No sooner did his broad green-tasselled hat and emerald cross appear at the corner of any street, than every human being, old and young, rich and poor, gentle and simple, rushed out of their houses, or across the road, to kneel and kiss his hand and receive his apostolical benediction, their faces all

the while beaming with a pleasure which it did
one's heart good to see. He first took her to the
great Jesuit college, opposite the Casa de las
Conchas, which contains upwards of 800 students.
It is a magnificent building, with a cloistered
gallery running round the roof, from whence the
view over the whole country is beautiful. The
church is a fine specimen of churrigueresque
work, with some pretty side chapels, and several
valuable pictures and relics. From thence they
went to the convent and church of the Augus-
tinians. The latter contains some very fine
pictures by Ribera—that great artist so little
known out of Spain—especially a 'Conception'
over the high altar. This church is exceedingly
rich in marbles and monuments, and in the Flo
rentine 'pietra dura' pulpit, St. Vincent of Ferrer
preached. Traversing the public gardens, now full
of flowers, from every corner of which the little
children ran forward to obtain the smile and
loving word of the good bishop, they came to
the discalced Carmelite convent, which is a little
outside the town, and where great joy at his
visit was shown by the nuns. This house, like
all the rest, was founded by the saint in great
poverty and difficulties. In her 'Life' there is
an amusing description of her arrival on the

Vigil of All Saints, 1570, and finding the house
full of students, who were with difficulty ejected;
the alarm of one of the nuns lest any stray ones
should be concealed in the garrets; and their
sleeping on straw, having found no sort of furniture or beds. Even later, when a chapel had
been built and dedicated to St. Joseph, St.
Theresa found that the rain came in on every
side, and threatened to put a stop to the con-
secration; but the storm passed away at the
prayers of the saint. She wrote at that time, 'In
none of the convents which our Lord allowed
us to found, have the nuns undergone greater
hardships than in this one.' But their faith
and patience triumphed over all. 'Ann of the
Incarnation' was the first prioress of this house,
and 'Anne of Jesus,' first mistress of novices.
These two ladies were cousins of St. Theresa, and
among the first to adopt her reform. Their portraits are in the parlour of this convent, and
'Anne of Jesus' has the sweetest and most saint-
like face that can be imagined. The rest of the
house, in its arrangements, discipline, and hermitages, is the same as all the others, and the
nuns have equally preserved her letters, and those
of St. John of the Cross, and of several of the
religious of the first foundation.

R

The English visitor confided to the bishop her great wish to visit Alva, the ' clôture ' of the whole to one interested in the life of St. Theresa, as there she died, and there the body of the saint rests.   But Alva is twelve miles from Salamanca, and neither carriage nor horses could be procured for the expedition.   The bishop directly solved the difficulty by offering her his episcopal coach and mules, which, after some hesitation and reluctance, she ventured at last to accept.   The next morning, therefore, after early mass at the beautiful Jesuit church, the two ladies started in solemn state for Alva, the only sad thing being the disappointment which their presence created in the villages, where the people, when they saw the episcopal equipage, rushed out of their houses to get the bishop's blessing, and saw instead nothing but two stupid women !   The vicar-general kindly accompanied them, the bishop being detained in Salamanca by the procession on St. Mark's-day. They passed by Arapiles, the scene of Wellington's great battle (called of Salamanca), in which he utterly defeated Marmont, and by which Madrid and Andalusia were saved.   Nothing but two low hills, one flat, the other conical, marks the spot immortalised by this great victory.   Alva is on the Tormes, and is approached through a fine natural ilex wood, and over a picturesque Roman bridge. Above the town towers the palace fortress of the dukes of Alva, now in ruins. But the episcopal mules, whose slow and stately pace had been the despair of our travellers ever since they left Salamanca, went straight to the Carmelite convent, which was evidently their usual destination. Here the curé, a kind and benevolent old man, met them, and, together with the vicar-general, desired to speak with the superior. This lady, evidently wearied with the number of pilgrims to the shrine of the saint, demurred greatly at the notion of admitting the strangers, and it required all the eloquence of the two priests, backed by the authority of the bishop and nunzio, and above all by the papal rescript, to obtain permission to enter the ' clausura.'

About two months after the foundation of Salamanca, St. Theresa was invited by Francis Velasquez, treasurer to the Duke of Alva and Teresa de Layz his wife, to found a house at Alva. These two people had long been praying in vain for children, when one night, in a dream, they saw a house, in the courtyard of which was a well and a corridor, and near it a green meadow full of beautiful flowers. By the well stood a saint-like man, who, pointing to the flowers, seemed to say to

them, 'These are far holier children than those
for whom you are longing.' A short time afterwards they removed to Alva, and when they came
to take possession of the house which had been
prepared for them, their astonishment was great at
recognising the very place they had seen in their
dream. There was the court, the well, the corridor, everything, except the saint! Perceiving the
hand of God in this matter, both Velasquez and
his wife determined to convert the house into a
convent, and asked St. Theresa to accept the
foundation. In accordance with their wish, St.
Theresa opened the house on the Feast of the
Conversion of St. Paul, under the title of the
'Incarnation.'

The visitors were taken first into her original
cell, and thence to the room in which she died:
the stones on which she sat, the bed on which she
was laid, all remain untouched. It was on the 3rd
of October, 1653, that, feeling her strength almost
entirely spent, she took leave of her religious, and
asked to receive the Holy Viaticum. When It
came, though previously unable to move, she
sprang up, and the love of her full heart burst
forth in the words : 'O Lord! the hour is come
which I have looked for these long, long years. It
is time, my Lord, that I should depart hence. Let

Thy most holy will be done. The end of my
weary exile is come at last, and my soul rejoices in
Thee, whom it has desired so ardently and so long.'
She repeated over and over again, 'After all, O
Lord, I am a *child of the Church,*' a thought which
seemed to fill her with unspeakable joy. Then she
said the Miserere, especially the verse, ' Cor con-
tritum et humiliatum Deus non despiciet,' which
she continued repeating as long as she had the
power of speech. She was asked where she would
wish to be buried. She answered quickly, ' Ought
I to have a will of my own ? ' and then added with
touching humility, ' Will they not give me a little
corner of earth here ? ' Mother Ann of St. Bartholomew never left her during the last days of
her life, and the saint died with her head resting
on her arm. A picture representing her death
hangs in this room, as also one of the vision in
which our Lord and His angels appeared at the
moment of her death at the foot of her bed to
escort the pure spirit up to heaven. There is also
a picture of her body as it appeared after death, in
her religious habit, over which had been thrown a
cloth of gold, exactly as she had seen in a dream
forty-eight years before ! The face had recovered
the youth and beauty of girlhood, and the com-
plexion had become white as alabaster. The body

was placed in a very deep grave, by desire of the foundress, who feared that it might one day be removed. Nine months after, it was taken up, and found as perfect and beautiful as the day of the burial. It was then conveyed to St. Joseph's convent at Avila, where, having been judicially examined, it was, by order of Pope Sixtus V., brought back to Alva, where it rests now over the high altar in a magnificent silver shrine. To this sanctuary our visitors were now led, through the choir, which contains likewise her heart in a crystal case, and a multitude of relics, pictures, and crucifixes, including the heads of St. Felix and St. Justus, brought from Rome, a quantity of the saint's letters and of Padre Garcia's, and a picture of St. John of the Cross, with the question of our Lord and his answer inscribed on the base :—

John, what recompense dost thou ask for thy labour ?
No other than to suffer and be condemned for Thy love, O Lord!

There are twenty-five religious in this house, which is one of the most interesting that can be seen in Spain. In the church are the bodies of Velasquez and his wife, the founders of the house, and of John de Ovalla and Doña Juana de Alhumada, the saint's favourite sister, whose monuments, with their child at their feet, are placed in a side transept. After spending the whole morn-

ing in this holy house, the two ladies went on to the
curé's, who had kindly prepared an excellent dinner for them, and received them in his little pres-
bytery with the frank and gentle courtesy which
is so characteristic of the Spaniards : only his hospitality was almost overwhelming ; his guests found
it impossible to eat and drink all the good things
which his generous heart had collected together in
their honour ! The evening saw them once more
at Salamanca, in the palace of the kind bishop to
whom they owed their deeply interesting Alva
visit. He took leave of them with fatherly tenderness, and at parting gave one of the ladies a
large and very admirable photograph of himself,
which she had much desired, but scarcely dared
ask for.

The peasants at Salamanca adhere to their old
national costume—the men with enormous hats,
the women, in addition to the bright yellow petticoats, with a kind of scarf or striped blanket, red,
white and black, which they throw over their
shoulders, or, if wet and cold, over the head :
this scarf seemed universal in the district. The
men had scarlet burnous, with heavy tasselled
fringes thrown picturesquely over one shoulder,
as at Valencia.

CHAPTER XII.

ZAMORA AND VALLADOLID.

At seven the next morning our travellers bade adieu to Salamanca, and went on by diligence to Zamora. The road is flat and uninteresting till you come to Corrales, where, to the left, in a sheltered valley, is Valparaiso, the once fine convent in which St. Ferdinand, that best of Spanish kings, was born. From the hermitage, called El Cristo de Morales, Zamora appears with its battlemented walls, fine cathedral, and picturesque old bridge with circular towers, which spans the Douro. The water of this river is said to be as nutritious as chicken-broth, 'Agua de Duero, caldo de pollos;' so runs the proverb. The peasants here use those dreadful carts (as in Portugal) with solid wheels—mere circles of wood without spokes or axles, which make the most abominable creaking noise that can be imagined; but their drivers never seem to find it out.

Our travellers were taken to a little 'posada' in the principal square, opposite a kind of Hôtel de Ville, with a beautiful Venetian façade, exquisite windows, and carved portals. The mistress of the house showed them into a room out of which was the universal box-bedstead recess; but they found it evidently occupied. Its owner, the colonel of the detachment of troops quartered there, came in a few minutes afterwards, and the ladies apologised for their unintentional intrusion, but were assured that he was delighted to place his apartment at their service, and in fact that there was no other. Presently a meal of some sort was announced to them, and our travellers no longer wondered at the colonel's choice of quarters. The uninviting dish of 'garbanzos' was brought up by a girl whose beauty will ever remain as an ideal in their minds. A perfectly oval face, the most tender lustrous eyes, a beautiful mouth, hair rolled above the delicately formed ear, behind which was stuck a bright pomegranate blossom—she would have made her fortune in six months as a model to a painter! and her shy, retiring, modest manner added to the wonderful charm of her appearance. At Cadiz, at Seville, and still more, in the outlying villages, beauty of this type had been met with by our party, but never in such perfection.

The train for Medina del Campo not starting for four or five hours, they resolved to employ their

time in exploring the curiosities of the town, and
first went to the cathedral, which has a curious
tower, fine Saxon arches and cloisters. The inside
has been modernised, but contains some beautiful
wood-carving in the choir and on the bishop's
throne, and some very fine monuments. But the
glory of Zamora is the Templar Church of Sta.
Magdalena. The deeply-recessed entrance, with its
remarkable circular arches enriched with Norman
and Moorish patterns, the rose-windows, and the
high altar, with its round arch and billet mouldings, are really unique in their beauty. The
'Alameda,' or public walk, begins opposite this
church, the space in the centre being filled with
roses, at that time in full blossom. From thence
there is a picturesque view of the old walls and of
the prison of the Cid, with the open cloister and
gallery of the bishop's palace, and the rich and
cultivated valley below. The hour for the departure of the train having now arrived, our travellers went down the hill to the station, their bags
being carried for them by the beautiful girl who
had so charmed them before, and who, refusing all
remuneration, shyly kissed the elder lady's hand
and vanished. Here was enacted one of those
scenes from real life which are often so much more
touching than the most exciting romance. A

young bride was starting with her husband, and
grouped round the railway carriage were all her
friends and old servants, to wish her good-bye.
One of the latter was her nurse, and the despair of
the poor woman was piteous to see.   Dressed in
her beautiful peasant's holiday costume, with
strings of pearls on her white bodice, but her face
swollen and disfigured by weeping, she clung to
her young mistress with a tenacity which was both
painful and touching.   The tie between masters
and servants in Spain is very close and very
sacred.   No one dreams of *ordering* their man or
maid to do anything; whatever is wanted must
be asked for with a deference and courtesy which
they consider their due, and which is invariably
accorded.   The servants consider themselves entirely as part of the family into which they enter,
and identify their interests, their sorrows, and
their joys, with those of their employers.

Our travellers arrived at Medina del Campo too
late to stop and visit the Carmelite convent there;
but were obliged to push on to Valladolid, which
they reached at eleven o'clock at night, very tired,
but charmed with their expedition.

Valladolid, once the capital of Spain, the birthplace of Philip II., and which witnessed likewise
the death of Columbus, has been entirely ruined by

the French, who sacked or destroyed everything
in it which was most interesting either in religion
or art. It is now being rebuilt in a stiff, commonplace way, and boulevards planted, as in a third-
rate French town. There is a great museum of
pictures, to which some of the party went, and
reported them, with very few exceptions, as exe-
crable. The cathedral was built by Herrera, the
architect of the Escurial, but was never finished.
It is cold and uninteresting to the last degree,
the only beautiful thing remaining in it being
the silver custodia.

The church of the Dominicans, called San
Pablo, was once a marvel of beauty and art;
but nothing now remains save the exquisite
façade. The fiat went forth from the Emperor
Bonaparte: 'Sa Majesté a ordonné la suppres-
sion du couvent des Dominicains, dans lequel
un Français a été tué.' The same fate awaited
the neighbouring college of San Gregorio, containing the wonderful 'retablo' of Juan de Juni:
the beautiful double cloisters alone remain. One
of the most interesting things in Valladolid, rarely
visited by travellers, is the house of the two
famous sculptors Juni and Hernandez, at the
corner of the Calle de San Luis. Juni was an
Italian, of the school of Michael Angelo, and
equally daring and grand in his conceptions.

Hernandez, who succeeded him both in his fame and in his studio, was the Murillo of Castilian sculpture. Like Angelico da Fiesole, he never began any work without prayer, and his whole creations breathe that same spirit of love and holiness which made an Englishman exclaim, on leaving Overbeck's studio one day in Rome : 'I feel as if I had been all the time in church.'

His private life was that of a brother of charity, and his name was a household word for all that was 'lovely and of good report.' Yet few care to go and see the little room which witnessed for twenty-three years that hidden life of piety and genius. The people in the house at present seemed utterly ignorant of the whole matter : the window of his studio is blocked up ; and his works are every day disappearing through the bad taste and indifference of his degenerate countrymen. Another interesting private house in Valladolid is the 'Casa del Sol,' now a barrack, once the residence of Gondomar, ambassador of Philip IV. to our James I., whose library was one of the most valuable in Spain. It contained a very curious collection of English literature of the time of Shakspeare. The whole was sold to Charles IV.; but as his Majesty did not pay, some 1,600 volumes were kept back and left to the tender mercies of the carpenter or bricklayer who had charge of the house ; and so these priceless treasures were finally sold for waste-paper and disappeared. Those seen by our travellers in the Queen's Library at Madrid formed only a small portion of his secret correspondence during his embassy in England. There are ten volumes there, and some others in the hands of the great antiquary, Señor Gayangos ; but as yet no authentic translation or account of their contents has reached this country, which is very much to be regretted.

The next visit of our travellers was to the bishop, whose palace contains a handsome staircase, cloistered 'patio,' and beautiful garden. He showed his guests, among other things, a very fine Murillo of the Crucifixion, and a beautiful 'retablo' by Pinturicchio, which he is having restored for his private chapel. His secretary volunteered to accompany one of the ladies to the Carmelite convent, while the rest continued their wanderings over the town. Entering into the parlour, while the superior was examining the permission to enter her 'clausura,' the lady's eyes fell on this quatrain over the door :—

> Hermano, una de dos :
> Ó no entrar, ó hablar de Dios.
> Que en la casa de Teresa
> Esta ciencia se profesa.

The original convent given by Bernardin of Mendoza, brother of the Bishop of Avila, was in an unhealthy situation near a river ; so that St. Theresa removed her nuns to the house where they now are, and which was purchased for them by his sister. It bears the title of 'Our Lady of Mount Carmel.' Mary of Ocampo (in religion called Maria de S. Juan Bautista) was the first prioress here, and trained her sisters to such perfection that St. Theresa spoke of the house as 'the most admirable of all her foundations.' It became the home of a perfect galaxy of saints, ladies of the highest rank and fortune devoting their lives to God in spite of all human difficulties and oppositions. The secret of their perfection is disclosed in the reply of one of them, to a person who was marvelling at her undisturbed tranquillity in the midst of severe trials and sufferings : 'The value of whatever we do and bear, however small it may be, for the love of God, is inestimable. We should not so much as turn our eyes, except to please Him.' This sanctity, and singleness of purpose, have descended like a precious heritage to the sisters now in the house. It was impossible not to be struck with the expression of their countenances. They have the usual mementoes of the saint : her letters, her clothes, her hair shirt, &c., and the MS. of her ' Camin de Perfeccion.' In the garden are hermitages, as at Avila : over the door of one is the inscription : ' At Carmel and at the Judgment Day, God only and I.' Philip II. decorated one of these little oratories, and placed in it an altar of ' azulejo ' work. They have also some very interesting pictures, portraits, crucifixes and relics.

The great trade of Valladolid is in silver-smith's work. With the discovery of a new world a vast quantity of silver and gold poured into Spain ; and this was wrought into beautiful forms and patterns by Antonio and Juan d'Arphe, Germans by origin and birth, but who settled at Valladolid, and executed almost all the beautiful cinquecento work which our travellers had seen in the different ecclesiastical treasuries of Spain. Juan became Master of the Mint at Sego-via, and published his designs for church plate, which have been generally adopted. Now, great artists and a taste for art seem to be equally extinct. But there is still a large manufacture of crosses, reliquaries, and the like in Valladolid, which are much sought after in other parts of Spain, like the silver buttons of Cordova and Granada.

It must be confessed, however, that Valladolid
was a disappointment to our travellers ; partly,
perhaps, because they had been spoiled by the
gorgeous beauty and antiquity of the south, but
also because the hand of the spoiler has really
left nothing but shells of buildings to testify to
the bygone glories of the ancient capital.

Without much regret, therefore, our travellers
went on the next day to Burgos, where many
things were yet unvisited by them. They arrived
late at night, and the next morning found one of
the party very early in the streets, enquiring the
way to the ' Iglesia Mayor.' She was directed to
a church a long way off in the heart of the town,
which turned out to be the very beautiful old
Benedictine Church of San Juan, instead of the
cathedral of which she was in search. It was,
however, well worth a visit, and contains some
very fine tombs of the Torquemada family. Service over, the lady wished to retrace her steps,
but then suddenly recollected that they had come
to a new hotel the night before, of which she
knew neither the name nor the address. The different turns she had taken in going to the church
had completely bewildered her small notions of
geography, and she could not ask her way, being
in the absurd position of not knowing what place

s

to ask for! In despair at last, after having wandered half over the town, she addressed herself to
a peasant woman sitting in a corner of one of
the streets, whose son was holding in his arms
one of those black and white lambs which always
bring to one's mind Murillo's picture of St. John
the Baptist. With the most ready and gentle
courtesy, the woman left her basket with a
neighbour, and undertook to guide the stranger
to the two or three principal hotels in the place
till they should find the right one—and this was
only a fresh proof, if one had been needed, of the
universal kindness which characterises the people.

Later in the day, our travellers returned to the
glorious cathedral, for which even their Toledo
and Seville experiences had not spoilt them;
and then went up the steps to the Church of
San Nicolas, which is on a steep ledge above, and
contains the most wonderfully carved 'retablo'
of every event in the life of the saint. It was
the finest and most delicate work of the sort
which they had seen in Spain. There were also
some interesting alabaster monuments in a side
chapel. From thence, ascending still higher,
they came to San Esteban, the oldest church in
Burgos, but which had been terribly knocked
about during the siege. A beautiful doorway and

Apostles' Door of Cathedral, Burgos.

rose-window, an internal gallery and pulpit, and
a fine old picture of the Last Supper in the
sacristy, are all that remain of its ancient splendour. The priest, seeing strangers in the church,
good-naturedly came forward and invited them to
come into the cloisters, from whence the view
over Burgos is very beautiful.

Descending the hill, they went to see several of
the old houses in Burgos : among others La Casa
del Cordon, the house of the constable, so called
from the rope over the portal, and the Casa de
Miranda, with its beautiful fluted pillars and
'patio.' But one thing was still unvisited, and that
was the Carmelite convent, the last of St. Theresa's
foundations, and one accomplished in spite of
contradictions and difficulties of all kinds. It was
on the 26th January, and therefore in the depth
of winter, with deep snow on the ground, and the
floods out in every direction, that the saint, though
already in failing health and strength, undertook
this work. She and her eight nuns were nearly
drowned in passing what is called 'The Bridges,'
near Burgos, the water having covered all the
tracks, so that the waggons were perpetually sink-
ing in the mire. In order to comfort her companions, St. Theresa showed no fear, but cheer-
fully exclaimed : 'Courage, my sisters ! What

greater happiness can you wish than, if need be, here to become martyrs for the love of our Lord? Suffering, through obedience, is a great and beautiful thing.' They arrived safely at the house of a devout widow lady, Catherine de Tolosa, who had purchased a building for their convent, and had already given up two of her daughters to be nuns under the saint's direction. Before their arrival they had obtained the consent both of the city and of the archbishop; but, to their dismay, found that the primate had changed his mind, and was now very much opposed to the new foundation, positively refusing permission for mass to be said in the house where they were. After weeks of vexatious delays, on the Vigil of St. Joseph, the archbishop granted the license. But now a fresh peril awaited them. The river rose and raged with such violence against the convent, that it threatened its total destruction. It flooded the lower storeys, so that they were obliged to remove everything up to the garrets; and they nearly died of hunger, no one being able to approach the house, and their stores being all buried beneath the waters. St. Theresa was very ill at the time, and said to Ann of St. Bartholomew: 'My child, I am fainting; see if you can find me a mouthful of bread.' One of the novices waded waist-deep into the water, and got her a loaf. At last two men swam to the house, and, diving under the water, broke open the doors to let it out of the rooms. The quantity of stones and rubbish left behind filled eight carts.

Such were the obstacles thrown in the way of this Burgos foundation ; but our saint's courage did not fail her, and the house remains to this day a monument of her loving faith in our Lord's promises. Speaking of the privations they had endured, she could still exclaim : 'Oh, my God! how little do fine buildings and exterior delights contribute to interior joy!'

The nuns received their unexpected visitor with immense kindness, and showed her everything in their house, inviting her to dine with them, and making a special ' tortilla ' (omelette) in her honour. They have some of the saint's letters, written in 1582, only one month before her death, and showed the stranger both these and the saint's cell, chair, dress, and writing materials, all of which have been preserved by them with the most filial veneration. Afterwards they took her into the choir, and sang while she played the harmonium for them, and a beautiful Benediction service concluded this her last visit to the Carmelite convents of Spain. If it be objected by some of our readers that too much stress has been laid upon the life of St. Theresa in a simple book of travels, the writer must give as the reason not only that one of the objects of her Spanish tour was an inspection of these convents, but that without understanding something of the history and inner life of one who has had so great an influence over the minds of her countrymen, it is almost impossible rightly to enter into the spirit of the people. She is the type of a character peculiar to Spain, and which could scarcely have existed in any other country; but its wonderful combination of spirituality and common sense makes her example the more invaluable to the age in which we live.

And now the sad day had come when our travellers' holiday was over, and they were compelled to leave Spain. Sorrowfully, for the last time, they drove under the massive old gateway of Burgos, with its turrets and statues, which has witnessed so many changes; and over the rapid river Arlanzon which skirts its walls. A couple of days' travel found them once more at the clean little inn of Bayonne, striving to reconcile themselves to the uniform French houses, French tongue, French climate, and French toilette, contrasting so painfully with their experiences of the last four months. They rested there a day, revisiting the cathedral, which, poor though it looked to their Spanish eyes, has been very prettily restored in the last few years; and then went for a short time to see the French sisters of charity at the great hospital established by the Mère Dévos. Some of her old sister-companions are still labouring there, and they saw her room, her bed, her place in the chapel, and the good Sœur Madeleine mentioned in her life, who had worked with her so indefatigably for ten years, and will labour on till God calls her to share the rest of her much-loved superior. Taking a little carriage in the afternoon, they drove over to Biarritz, that bright little watering-place, with its picturesque rocks jutting out into the sea, which roars under its tiny caverns, its nice smooth sands, and its white image of the 'Star of the Sea' standing on the extreme point of the little pier. Though it was not a regular show-day, the presentation of their cards obtained admission for our travellers to the emperor's palace, which is like an ordinary private gentleman's house, very simple and very comfortable. The empress's bed-room, fitted up with a gay linen chintz, contains but two little pictures, one of the Blessed Virgin, the other of St. Vincent de Paul, which hangs over her bed.

The gardens slope down to the sea, and she has just built in the grounds a beautiful little chapel, thoroughly Spanish in its decorations, with Moorish coloured roof and ' azulejo' walls, and the choir or tiny apse beautifully painted, the subject being the Blessed Virgin, surrounded by angels, with a background of ' white lilies and vermilion roses.' This was our travellers' last reminiscence of Spain —a country which they left with the greatest regret, and with the earnest hope of revisiting it before the so-called march of civilisation has utterly destroyed all that is beautiful, simple, and characteristic of this noble people.

APPENDIX.

SEMANA SANTA EN SEVILLA.

ENTRE las ciudades que más se han distinguido en el orbe cristiano por la grandeza de sus cultos, figura la Capital de Andalucía; contribuyendo á este éxito la veneranda antigüedad de su devocion á representar los augustos misterios de la redencion humana con procesiones y ostentosas ritualidades, el brillo que comunicaron á estas ceremonias la esplendidez de su ilustre aristocrácia, lo píngue de su comercio, y el fervor de sus cuerpos gremiales, al par del incentivo poderoso que añadió á tan célebres festividades el concurso de tantos artistas esclarecidos como enriquecieron con admirables obras de escultura las lujosas andas presentadas por las Hermandades á la adoracion de un vecindario eminentemente católico.

El orígen de las cofradías se remonta á los fastos honrosos de los gremios, los cuales, obedeciendo á la inspiracion religiosa para consagrar debidamente sus asociaciones, erigieron magníficos santuarios, hospitales y casas de misericordia, rivalizando en públicas muestras de piedad con las hermandades instituidas por los caballeros y ricos tratantes en el comercio de las Indias Occidentales. El espíritu de las épocas y el carácter particular de un pueblo de tan ardiente fantasía esplican las escenas místicas que mostraron un tiempo las procesiones de penitencia y su acertada supresion por incompatibles con el lustre y severidad del culto.

En nuestros dias la Semana Santa conserva sus sagrados recuerdos y representa al vivo esa armonía maravillosa de la religion cristiana con el estado civil; refluyendo el rito en pró de las artes, industrias, ciencias y tráfico, á quienes paga con creces el auxilio que prestan á sus solemnidades.

DIVINOS OFICIOS EN LA SANTA IGLESIA METRO-POLITANA.

Nuestra insigne y famosa basílica, correspondiendo á sus tradiciones, á la religiosidad nunca desmentida de su Cabildo y á su celo del esplendor de la Metrópoli, no ha perdonado sacrificio por continuar en este año el ritual solemnísimo que atrae á los fieles á su sagrado recinto. El Emmo. Prelado de esta Diócesis, coadyuvando solícito á tan augustos fines, esfuerza á pesar de su quebrantada salud la magnificencia de las ceremonias con que recuerda la Iglesia los misterios de la pasion de Jesucristo.

Los oficios del Domingo de Ramos principiarán á las seis de la mañana. Despues de tercia bendice el Sr. Dean las palmas y olivas y sale el Ilmo. Cabildo Eclesiástico en procesion por Gradas. Al regresar al Templo, el subdiácono dá con el asta de la cruz un golpe en la puerta contigua á la Giralda, para significar que el Redentor con la suya nos abrió las del cielo. Concluida esta ceremonia predica el Sr. Canónigo Magistral; cantándose luego la misa y la pasion con acompañamiento de música. Por la tarde se hace la misteriosa ostension de la sagrada bandera.

En los del Mártes y Miércoles Santos se canta tambien la pasion con la misma solemnidad; rompiéndose en la del segundo el velo blanco con estrepitosos truenos. En las vísperas se hace la última ostension de la sagrada bandera. Terminan las tinieblas con un solemne Miserere de nueve á diez de la noche y acto contínuo se conduce en procesion el Santísimo Sacramento á la capilla del Sagrario.

El Juéves Santo empieza á las nueve el augusto sacrificio de la misa. El clero comulga en ella y luego deposita la sagrada forma en el magnífico monumento que se erige en la sétima bóveda del trascoro sobre la sepultura de D. Fernando Colon, hijo del descubridor del nuevo mundo. Trazó tan maravilloso proyecto Antonio Florentin en el año 1545; concluyéndose en 1554 y sus reformas posteriores en 1689. El monumento tiene la altura de 40 varas, es enteramente aislado y consta de cuatro cuerpos, presentando cuatro frentes iguales con la planta de una cruz griega. Sobre 16 pedestales de 9 pies se elevan otras tantas columnas de 22 de alto y tres de diámetro y en grupos de cuatro sostienen su arquitrave, friso y cornisa. Dentro de este primer cuerpo aparece otro pequeño, que lo forman otras cuatro columnas y bajo una cúpula con ricos adornos ostenta su gallardia la famosa custodia de Juan de Arfe con una urna de oro, donde se coloca el Santísimo Sacramento. Imita la blancura del alabastro, esmaltado de oro en labores, filetes, perfiles é inscripciones. Ciento cuarenta lámparas de plata, diez y seis blandones gigantescos del propio metal y 581 luces de cera iluminan tan suntuosa obra.

Diez y seis columnas del Templo se visten con una riquísima colgadura de terciopelo carmesí y anchos galones de oro, apareciendo igual adorno en todo el espacio de la puerta grande.

Su Eminencia sirve á las doce una espléndida comida á trece pobres, vestidos á su costa. Las mesas están de manifiesto al público en el palacio Arzobispal desde por la mañana hasta que acaban los oficios.

Á las tres de la tarde lava el Sr. Dean los pies á los referidos pobres en la crujía del coro al presbiterio; continuan las completas y las tinieblas que concluyen á las diez de la noche y entónces se repiten las patéticas entonaciones del Miserere, que como el que se canta en la anterior, puso en música el maestro Eslaba y cuyas notas, admiracion de propios y estraños, llenan de melodías delicadas y armonías sorprendentes las magestuosas bóvedas del Templo.

El Viernes Santo á las seis predica un Misionero junto al Monumento. Acto contínuo empiezan las horas canónicas, cántase la pasion y el celebrante pide misericordia para todos los hombres y ostenta solemnemente la Cruz á la adoracion del pueblo. Despues se forma la procesion al Monumento y vuelve con la Divina Magestad á la capilla mayor donde termina el rito de la mañana; principiándose las tinieblas por la tarde á las tres y media.

Los oficios del Sábado Santo comienzan á las siete por la bendicion del fuego nuevo y la del cirio Pascual, que en todos tiempos se ha reconocido como símbolo de la resurreccion del Salvador. Acto seguido se cantan doce profecías para instruccion de los catecúmenos; se bendice la pila bautismal; entónanse las letanías de los santos; continúa la misa y se descubre el retablo al GLORIA IN EXCELSIS DEO enmedio de truenos y con un repique general de campanas, que interrumpe el piadoso silencio de tan solemnes dias.

Aumentará el esplendor de la Semana Santa la estacion á la Iglesia Catedral de las siguientes Cofradías.

DOMINGO DE RAMOS.

Santo Cristo del Silencio, desprecio de Herodes y Ntra. Señora de la Amargura.—Parroquia de S. Juan Bautista.

El Tribunal de Herodes en el acto de mandar que Jesus fuese conducido con la vestidura blanca á la presencia de Pilatos, representa el primer paso de esta Cofradía. La escultura del Señor es obra de Pedro Roldan; dos de los soldados romanos son de Pedro Duque Cornejo, constructor de la célebre silleria del coro de la Catedral de Córdoba; otros dos y Herodes se deben á D. Benito Hita del Castillo. Las andas son modernas, de órden corintio, con los Evangelistas en los ángulos, cuatro medallones de medio relieve en los centros, recordando pasages del antiguo y nuevo Testamento, diez y seis profetas y varias alegorías. En el segundo paso aparece la Santísima Vírgen bajo pálio y con profusion de luces, acompañada de S. Juan, cuya famosa efigie esculpieron con mucha fortuna los cinceles del susodicho Hita del Castillo. Las túnicas de los nazarenos que preceden al primero son blancas, y negras las de los que van ante el segundo.

Sagrada Entrada en Jerusalen, Santo Cristo del Amor y Ntra.
Señora del Socorro.—Parroquia de S. Miguel.

Lleva esta Cofradía tres pasos. Representa el primero la entrada triunfante del Salvador en la ciudad Santa; acompañado á su sagrada efigie los apóstoles S. Pedro, S. Juan y Santiago. Delante aparecen arrodillados seis hebreos, tendiendo sus capas, para que las pise el Señor y al lado una palma. El segundo conduce al Crucificado exhalando el último suspiro. Los músculos violentamente contraidos, la lividéz del semblante y la expresion de los ojos, dán una idea admirable de la agonía del Redentor y prueban el acierto del insigne Juan Martinez Montañés en sus obras. El tercer paso, sobre peana dorada y bajo pálio de terciopelo bordado de oro, sostenido por doce varas de plata, ostenta á la imágen dolorosa de nuestra Señora del Socorro, con multitud de alhajas y candelabros.

MIÉRCOLES SANTO.

Santo Cristo de la Columna y Azotes y Madre de Dios de la Victoria.
Iglesia de los Terceros.

Desde 1846 dejó de hacer estacion esta Hermandad; pero á impulsos de una ardiente devocion y venciendo multitud de obstáculos han logrado sus individuos, pertenecientes á una clase honrada de artesanos, ofrecer en el presente año á la adoracion de los fieles las imágenes de su instituto. El primer paso conduce, sobre peana antigua delicadamente tallada y con ricos adornos dorados, á Ntro. Sr. Jesucristo amarrado á una columna y dos judíos azotándolo. En el segundo aparece bajo pálio la Santísima Vírgen con piedras preciosas y saya y manto bordados de oro; atribuyéndose, tanto esta distinguida escultura, como las otras de la misma Cofradía, á los discípulos del celebre Roldan. La tristeza del primer asunto y la dulzura y resignacion espresadas con feliz verdad en el rostro de la amorosa Madre de Dios, conmueven tiernamente el ánimo y lo inducen á contemplar con recojimiento sus acerbos dolores.

Santo Cristo de las Siete Palabras y María Santísima de los Remedios.
Iglesia de Ntra. Señora del Cármen.

El Calvario con el Redentor crucificado y en actitud de pronunciar sus últimas palabras, la Santísima Vírgen, S. Juan y la Magdalena al pié de la Cruz, representa el único paso de esta Cofradía. Las imágenes son de aventajados escultores, entre los cuales figura el jóven D. Manuel Gutierrez, y merced á los esfuerzos piadosos de los nuevos hermanos estrenan trajes de terciopelo. Serán conducidas sobre una peana dorada con tableros diestramente tallados y primorosos adornos ; coronando sus ángulos ángeles mancebos con grupos de luces.

JUEVES SANTO.

Sagrada Oracion del Huerto y María Santísima del Rosario, en sus
Misterios Dolorosos.—Iglesia de Monte-Sion.

Aparece en el primer paso Nuestro Padre Jesus orando de rodillas delante del Angel, que con el Cáliz y la Cruz se eleva sobre un trono de nubes, junto á una palmera. Al frente se vé la puerta del huerto de Gethsemani, detras de la cual duermen los apóstoles S. Juan, S. Pedro y Santiago. El zócalo, restaurado con mucho gusto en este año, es de bastante mérito. Todas las efigies son del célebre escultor sevillano Pedro Roldan, excepto el Angel y los medallones de la peana, que la tradicion atribuye á su hija Luisa, conocida con el nombre de la Roldana. Figura este misterio, con una propiedad interesantísima, una de las mas dolorosas escenas de la pasion del Hombre-Dios. El pensamiento se transporta á aquella memorable noche, víspera de la redencion del mundo, y al batir de los penachos de la gentil palmera, se imagina al Salvador *retrocediendo un instante ante la sombra espantosa de la muerte,* segun una poética frase, y exclamando : *que pase lejos de mí este cáliz.*

En otras andas sale bajo pálio la Santísima Vírgen, con un rico manto de terciopelo cubierto de estrellas de oro de alto relieve, ostentando alhajas de gran valor y considerable número de candelas. Los nazarenos visten túnicas blancas y mantos negros de lana, y entre otras insignias estrena esta Cofradía un *Senatus* enteramente igual al que usaban las legiones romanas.

Dulce Nombre de Jesus, Sagrado Descendimiento de Ntro. Señor
Jesucristo, y Quinta Angustia de María Santísima.—Parroquia de
Santa María Magdalena.

Dos pasos suntuosos lleva esta Cofradía. El primero representa la aceptacion del cruento sacrificio, para redimir al hombre del pecado

Osténtase magestuosamente sobre una elevada colina la efigie del divino Nazareno en su infancia, obra maravillosa del célebre escultor Gerónimo de Hernandez, bendiciendo los atributos principales de la Pasion, reverentemente ofrecidos por un grupo de ángeles. Al pié se distingue el Santo Precursor, anunciando á las generaciones, figuradas por graciosos párvulos, entretenidos en juegos infantiles, la mision augusta que el verbo humanado vino á desempeñar lleno de generoso interés por la salvacion de las almas. Preciosos corderos, símbolo del rebaño de Cristo, acuden á beber las cristalinas aguas de la Salud eterna, que descienden de la cumbre; divisándose en segundo término un árbol alegórico al del fruto prohibido, con una serpiente ya exánime por la aparicion de Jesus. La montaña, apesar de sus grandes dimensiones, ofrece mucha ligereza por sus acertadas quiebras embellecidas por los arbustos, flores y plantas aromáticas, que embalsaman el aire con su fragancia. La inspiracion de esta obra y las nuevas esculturas son hijas de la acreditada inteligencia de dos artistas contemporáneos, cuyos nombres recordará la posteridad con aplauso.

Los santos varones José y Nicodemus en los extremos superiores de las escaleras y apoyados en los brazos de la Cruz, que presenta á la veneracion pública el segundo paso, suspenden con fajas de lienzo el cuerpo de Jesus difunto, en el acto del descendimiento. Junto al árbol sagrado aparecen Nuestra Señora de la Quinta Angustia, así titulada por la que padeció en este trance; S. Juan Evangelista, la Magdalena y las Santas Mugeres con sábanas de riquísima tela para recibir el cadáver del Redentor, cuyo descenso parece que se presencia realmente, por el efecto admirable que causa en los que lo contemplan el movimiento de la dolorosa efigie, balanceándose en el aire, pendiente de las ligaduras que sujetan las manos de los varones. Las esculturas dan honra por su relevante mérito al ingenio del fecundo Pedro Roldan. Las imágenes lucen magníficos trajes de terciopelo con espléndidos bordados de oro, formando dibujos elegantes, que se extienden por toda la tela, y las peanas de las andas son de mucho gusto con altos relieves. Los nazarenos usan túnicas moradas con mantos blancos y todas las insignias de esta Hermandad corresponden al brillo de sus cultos.

Nuestro Padre Jesus de la Pasion y María Santísima de la Merced.
Parroquia de S. Miguel.

Sobre una peana dibujada por el inteligente adornista D. Juan Rossi, construida y dorada con singular esmero en sus talleres, aparece, vistiendo túnica de terciopelo con bordados de oro, la bellísima efigie del

Nazareno, obra maravillosa del famoso escultor Juan Martinez Montañés, quien, segun refiere Arana de Varflora en sus 'Hijos de Sevilla,' *salia á encontrarla por las calles cuando la sacaban en procesion, diciendo que era imposible hubiese él ejecutado cosa tan admirable.* Lleva el Señor la Cruz al hombro con la ayuda del Cirineo, que se atribuye al mismo autor, siendo, por su expresiva naturalidad, de las mejores esculturas de su clase. Cuatro ángeles estofados sobresalen en los ángulos del zócalo y en su centro escudos esmaltados de órdenes religiosas.

En otras andas salen con lujosísimos trajes, recamados de oro, la devota efigie de Nuestra Señora y la de S. Juan Evangelista bajo pálio, con varas y cornisa de plata, siendo del propio metal su moderna peana. Profusion de alhajas y de luces, en vistosos candelabros, dán mayor realce á este paso. Los nazarenos visten túnicas blancas con antifáz morado.

VIERNES DE MADRUGADA.

Jesus Nazareno, Santa Cruz en Jerusalen y María Santísima de la Concepcion.—Iglesia de S. Antonio Abad.

Esta Cofradía, primera que juró defender la Pureza de la Vírgen, se distingue por la rígida observancia de su instituto y por el piadoso recogimiento de sus nazarenos al hacer estacion á la Sta. Iglesia. Lleva dos pasos: en el primero, últimamente restaurado, sale el Señor con una cruz de carey al hombro, ofrenda del comercio de las Indias, llevando una riquísima túnica bordada de oro. A los lados se encuentran dos ángeles mancebos muy bellos, con faroles de plata y candelabros en los ángulos.

En el segundo aparecen sobre una peana de plata la Vírgen Santísima y S. Juan Evangelista bajo pálio de terciopelo salpicado de estrellas y sostenido por varas del propio metal; luciendo multitud de reliquias, macetas y ramos tambien de plata, con profusion de bujías en candeleros. La imágen del Nazareno es antiquísima y las otras dos se ejecutaron por Cristóbal Ramos, reconociéndose en todas ellas no escaso mérito.

Nuestro Padre Jesus del Gran Poder y María Santísima del Mayor Dolor y Traspaso.—Parroquia de S. Lorenzo.

Su primer paso, ostenta la sagrada efigie del Redentor, llevando sobre sus hombros el grave peso de la Cruz en actitud de caminar hácia el

Gólgota, donde debia consumarse el divino sacrificio. Escultura del eminente artista Juan Martinez Montañés. La expresion del rostro recuerda la escuela de Murillo en la verdad pasmosa, con que traduce el alma de los santos. La peana figura un elegante canasto calado de riquísima talla, y su perfil es de tanto gusto que, á pesar de su excesivo tamaño, hace ligera y graciosa la inimitable combinacion de sus contornos. Los ángeles y relieves, que adornan el referido zócalo, son tambien de imponderable mérito.

Ocupan el segundo las imágenes de la Vírgen Santísima y del discípulo querido, obra del mismo autor, viendo con hondísima pena el tránsito de Jesus al Calvario. Todas tres efigies visten túnicas y mantos de terciopelo, espléndidamente bordados de oro; brillando en las últimas andas alhajas de inmenso valor y profusion de luces. Distínguese tambien esta Cofradía por el órden y devocion de sus hermanos.

Sentencia de Cristo y María Santísima de la Esperanza.—Parroquia de S. Gil.

El Tribunal de Pilatos, en el acto de pronunciar su sentencia, es el asunto del primer paso. Pilatos aparece sentado en el testero, bajo un dosel de madera tallada y delante los ministros en sus respectivos asientos. Enmedio se vé al Redentor con las manos ligadas y dos judios armados, que lo tienen preso. Á los lados del trono de Pilatos se encuentran dos criados, uno con palangana y otro con el jarro y la toalla para lavarse las manos. La riqueza de la peana, hábilmente construida por el tallista D. José Vicente Hernandez, honra al arte y muestra el fervoroso celo de los cofrades. Bajo pálio de plata sale en otras andas la Santísima Vírgen, engalanada con un magnífico manto y saya de terciopelo, luciendo profusos y lujosísimos bordados de oro. Las efigies principales son de Roldan. Los nazarenos llevan túnicas blancas con antifáz verde y acompañará á una numerosa escolta de milicia romana, ricamente vestida, su correspondiente música con trajes análogos. Conserva esta Cofradía la ceremonia de la humillacion, que se verifica en el campo de la Macarena al regresar á su iglesia.

POR LA TARDE.

Santísima Cruz en el Monte Calvario y Ntra. Señora de la Soledad. Iglesia de S. Buenaventura.

Presenta el único paso de esta ilustre hermandad á la Santísima Vírgen al pié de la Cruz, sintiendo en su soledad amarga la muerte de

T

su querido Hijo. El árbol sagrado ostenta las escaleras y el sudario con que lo descendieron los Santos Varones. La efigie luce un precioso manto de terciopelo bordado de oro, y se debe á los cinceles del distinguido artista D. Gabriel Astorga ; siendo la peana de mucho gusto, con bajos relieves y atributos de la pasion en medallones.

Santísimo Cristo de la Exaltacion y Ntra. Sra. de las Lágrimas.
Parroquia de Sta. Catalina.

Aparece en el primer paso el Salvador de nuestras almas, ya enclavado en la Cruz, cuya elevacion procuran cuatro verdugos, para erigirla en el hueco de una peña. Es devotísima la actitud del Señor y aflictiva la de los ladrones, los cuales manifiestan en sus semblantes el dolor que les causa el tormento y la idea de su próxima muerte. Dos ministros de justicia á caballo presencian tan angustiosa escena ; atribuyéndose las esculturas á la acreditada inteligencia de Pedro Roldan. La peana es nueva, embelleciéndola delicados adornos de talla dorada sobre fondo blanco y escudos de órdenes religiosas, pintados con la propiedad heráldica que distingue á las obras del profesor D. José Diaz. El segundo lleva á la Santísima Vírgen, estrenando una saya y un manto ricamente bordados de oro, sobre peana de plata y bajo pálio, que sostienen diez varas del mismo metal, adornándolo candelabros y otros objetos preciosos, con crecido número de bujías. Los nazarenos visten túnicas blancas con antifáz morado.

Santo Cristo de la Conversion del Buen Ladron y María Santísima de Monserrate.—Parroquia de Santa María Magdalena.

Esta Cofradía, notable por su ostentosa restauracion, decora con inmensa esplendidez sus pasos. El primero conduce á S. Isaias Profeta, sentado bajo una esbelta palmera de plata, en el acto de escribir la venida pasion y muerte de Cristo. El segundo representa al Señor crucificado, en el instante de ofrecer el paraiso al buen ladron en premio de su reconocimiento. Esta escultura es una de las obras mas insignes del célebre Montañés. Al pié de la Cruz figura la Magdalena en actitud de abrazarla. Las peanas forradas de terciopelo, lucen ricos ardornos dorados ; coronando los ángulos ángeles y candelabros de mucho mérito. El tercero ostenta bajo pálio de plata á la Santísima Vírgen con saya de terciopelo blanco profusamente bordada de oro y suntuoso manto azul de la misma tela, guarnecido de dos anchas franjas y recamado de oro en el fondo, brillando el escudo de la Corporacion en la cola que recogen sacerdotes. Dos magníficos candelabros de plata iluminan la parte posterior del paso, cuyas andas van cubiertas con caidas de terciopelo azul tambien bordadas de oro y plata. Estotra efigie es igualmente de Montañés, y entre la pedrería con que la adornan se vé el aderezo regalado por la Reina Doña Maria Amelia, apareciendo á sus pies multitud de reliquias, alhajas y candeleros. Una magnífica banda de música con lujosos vestidos á la romana precederá á la centuria que custodia el segundo paso, representándose la Fé y la Muger Verónica por jóvenes con preciosos trajes análogos. Los nazarenos visten túnicas blancas con antifáz azul.

Sagrada Mortaja de Nuestro Señor Jesucristo y María Santísima de la Piedad.—Parroquia de Sta. Marina.

Nuestro Padre Jesus descendido de la Cruz, la Santísima Vírgen, S. Juan, las tres Marías y los Santos Varones reunidos en el Calvario al pié de la Cruz en actitud de subir el cuerpo del Señor con el sudario, primorosamente sembrado de flores para colocarlo en el sepulcro, forman el único paso de esta Cofradía. Su zócalo figura un canasto con relieves y medallones dorados que recuerdan asuntos de la pasion y lleva seis magníficos candelabros. Las efigies son de Pedro Roldan y la de Ntra. Sra. estrena un rico manto bordado de oro. Los nazarenos irán con nuevas túnicas moradas y mantos negros de merino, rodeando las andas sacerdotes con estolas. El doloroso aspecto de aquellas sagradas imágenes en el Gólgota, produce en el ánimo una profunda melancolía y agolpa á los párpados el llanto.

Nuestra Señora de la Soledad.—Parroquia de S. Miguel.

Esta Cofradía, cuyos cultos tuvieron una ostentacion estraordinaria, redobla sus afanes para mantener su antiguo lustre. Lleva dos pasos: uno con la Cruz, separado ya el cuerpo sacrosanto del Redentor, y otro con la Santísima Vírgen, llorando en su amargo aislamiento la intensidad de su pena. Bajo pálio, sostenido por varas de plata, aparece esta sagrada efigie, vestida de terciopelo con relieves bordados de oro. Los hermanos usan túnicas blancas con antifáz negro.

El órden seguido en la presente descripcion, no limita las facultades de las jurisdicciones eclesiástica y civil para fijar definitivamente el que deban guardar las Cofradías en su estacion á la Basílica Metropolitana. Todavía es posible que tenga aumento su número, porque las hermandades no comprendidas en este manifiesto pueden resolver su salida antes del Mártes Santo.

Excúsase inculcar al pueblo de Sevilla el espíritu de piadoso recogimiento propio de tan solemne época, porque la cultura del vecindario es uno de los timbres que justamente lo enorgullecen, mereciendo la entera confianza de sus autoridades.

Sevilla, 20 de Marzo de 1866.

El Presidente del Excmo. Ayuntamiento,
Joaquin de Peralta.

José Elias Fernandez,
Secretario.

PLAZA DE TOROS DE SEVILLA.

CON PERMISO DEL EXCMO. SR. GOBERNADOR DE ESTA PROVINCIA.

DOS GRANDES CORRIDAS DE TOROS

en las tardes de los dias 18 y 19 del presente mes de Abril de 1866 (si el tiempo no las impide).—2ª. y 3ª. DE ABONO.

La plaza será presidida por la Autoridad competente.

Los Doce Toros que han de lidiarse pertenecen á las ganaderías siguientes :—

Dia 18. Seis de la del Sr. D. José Arias de Saavedra de Utrera, hoy de la propiedad del Excmo. Sr. D. Ildefonso Nuñez de Prado de Arcos de la Frontera.

Dia 19. Seis de la de la Señora Doña Josefa Fernandez Viuda de Miura, de Sevilla.

ESPADAS.

Francisco Arjona Guillen (CUCHARES), de Madrid; Antonio Sanchez (EL TATO) y Manuel Carmona, ambos de Sevilla; los que matarán alternando.

Sobresaliente de espada.—FRANCISCO ARJONA REYES, de Sevilla.

PICADORES.—Manuel Ledesma (el Coriano); Francisco Calderon, de Alcalá de Guadaira; Antonio Pinto, de Utrera; Miguel Alanis, de Dos-Hermanas, Ramon Fernandez (el Esterero), de Madrid; Francisco Rodas y Juan Trigo, de Sevilla; trabajando este último en la tarde del 18 y Miguel Alanís en la del 19. Si los picadores anunciados se inutilizan no exigirá el público otros aunque queden toros por lidiar.

BANDERILLEROS.—Matías Muñiz, Pablo Herraiz, Juan Sanchez (no Teveas) y Mariano Anton, todos de Madrid; Francisco Ortega (el Cuco), de Cádiz; José Gomez (el Gallito), y José Martin, ambos de Sevilla.

CACHETEROS.—Manuel Bustamante (Pulga) y Manuel Gallango, de Sevilla.

PREVENCIONES DE LA AUTORIDAD.—Siguen las establecidas para el órden y gobierno de la plaza. Se usará de banderillas de fuego para los toros que no tomen varas y para los que disponga la Presidencia, habiendo preparados perros de presa para los casos que la misma juzgue oportunos. No se permitirá la entrada por las puertas de las cuadras mas que ha lidiadores y operarios. Bajo ningun pretesto se tomará dinero en las puertas. Todo billete que no se encuentre signado con el sello de la Empresa, será considerado como ilegítimo. Por disposicion de la Autoridad superior queda espresamente prohibido que persona alguna solicite permiso para la ejecucion de ninguna clase de suertes durante las corridas.

NOTAS.—Los vendedores de frutas, dulces, gaseosas y demas, entrarán esclusivamente por la puerta del Principe con billete de sombra. Á los aguadores se les espenderán billetes al precio de 4 reales, á las 7 de la mañana de los dias de las corridas en la sala de Diputacion de la plaza de Toros, siendo la puerta de entrada para aquellos la del Principe y hora de la una de la tarde. Los despachos de billetes se situarán en la calle de Génova, Campana, Dados, Imágen y Plaza de Toros, abriéndose á las seis de la mañana de los dias de las funciones, retirándose de dichos puntos á las dos de la tarde para ocupar los de los alrededores de la plaza. Una bánda de música compuesta de los mejores profesores y bajo la direccion de D. Antonio Palatin, tocará piezas escogidas media hora antes de empezarse las corridas y en los intermedios. Los toros se encontrarán en Tablada las tardes vispera de las funciones.

Las localidades de preferencia para ambas corridas se espenderán en contaduría con el aumento de dos reales, desde las diez de la mañana de los dias 16 y 17 hasta las tres de la tarde de cada uno de ellos, en la calle Tetuan núm. 27 y en los dias de las corridas en los despachos de calle Génova y Campana al precio de tarifa.

La plaza se abrirá á la UNA Y MEDIA, empezando las corridas á las CUATRO en punto.

TARIFA.—Delanteros de palcos altos y bajos, Rvn. 34.—Segundas de id., 20.—Barandillas de piedra, 24.—Barandillas de Diputacion y asientos de Toril, 20.—Id. de cajon, 30.—Id. de vallas, 15.—Centros de piedra, 12.—Id. de Diputacion, 10.—Sombra, 9.—Sol, 6.

LA MULETA.

REVISTA TAURINA MADRILEÑA.

TERCERA media corrida de toros, verificada hoy 15 de Abril, en la que se corrieron tres de Don Justo Hernandez, vecino de Madrid, y otros tres del Excmo. Sr. Marqués del Saltillo que lo es de Carmona.

Salió el primero de Hernandez, llamado *Pandereto*, retinto, oscuro, ojinegro, bien armado, boyante y de libras, duro al hierro y rematando. Tomó cuatro varas y un marronazo de Pinto, sufriendo dos caidas é hiriéndole el penco, y seis de Onofre, dándoles dos caidas de *padre y muy señor mio.*

El inteligente Muñiz le clavó dos pares cuarteando, y otro el Cuquito á topa-carnero con grandes aplausos; sentido el vicho al castigo, se huyó á las tablas; el Tato armado con los *trastos* lo pasó con gran trabajo por haberse hecho receloso y tapiarle la salida al diestro; y despues de ocho naturales y cuatro con la derecha, le dió muerte de una magnífica á volapié en los tres Ochavos.

De Lesaca fué el segundo, llamado *Capucha*, negro, meano, algo corni pasó y de cabeza, sintiéndose al hierro y haciéndose tardo. Tres veces le clavó la pica Onofre, dándole un marronazo y sufriendo dos caidas, con pérdida de un caballo, y dos de Pinto, con otro marronazo con su correspondiente *costalazo* y pérdida del *pitillo* que montaba.

Los Banderilleros Yust y Chesin le clavaron tres pares de palos al cuarteo.

Tocaron á muerte, y el Gordito que á manera de hacerle cuadra y partir derecho, despues de diez pasos naturales y un cambio, por puro lujo, le mandó á mejor vida de una buena, cuarteando en el embroque.

Brincó el tercero en el circo, de nombre *Comisario*, de la ganadería de Hernandez, retinto, súcio, ojo de perdiz, bien armado. Salió avanto, parándose y creciéndose al *palo*.

Cuatro veces le *pinchó* Pinto (el cerviguillo), matándole un jamelgo, otras tantas por la de Onofre, y dos del reserva (francés) muy bien puestas, agradando al público que justamente le aplaudió.

Este picador nos parece que promete, no obstante lo poco que le hemos visto trabajar.

Tocaron banderillas, y Jaqueta le colgó en lo bueno dos pares de frente y uno Villaviciosa, cuarteando.

El vicho se huyó al castigo, escupiéndose al trapo y haciéndose de sentido, y lo mató Lagartijo despues de varios pases, sin concluir de un golletazo, dándole las tablas.

—Sor Lagartijo para matar toros hay que parar los pies y arrancar corto y derecho.

Lesaqueño fué el cuarto, llamado *Ligero*, correspondiendo á su nombre, salió *arrancao*, era de pelo negro, meano, cornicorto, brabucon y blando sin rematar la lidia. El brazo *férreo* del picador Pinto, le hizo huir al castigo á la segunda vara, despues de otra de Onofre.

Tomaron los rehiletes Mariano Anton y Muñiz, clavándole dos pares por mitad, uno al cuartéo de Mariano y otro *Barrian* de Muñiz, metiéndose en la cuna.

Aun cuando este *vicho* se habia hecho receloso, tomó los *avios* el Tato y empajándole en el trapo le compuso algo la cabeza; pero arrancándole con bastante *asco*, le dió un pinchazo saliendo el *vicho* detrás. Volvió á pasarlo otras mil veces y sin tener en cuenta que el vicho le tenia ganado el terreno por no estar *igualado* lo pinchó de nuevo, saliendo arrollado y viéndose obligado á abandonar otra vez al trapo. Continuó la faena pinchándolo cuatro veces más, callendo descabellado del último (silva descomunal y toques *Chironescos*).

De nombre *Pinturero* fué el quinto, de pelo retinto, oscuro, negro y bien armado. Salió como el *aire*, tomando dos varas á la carrera de los dos picadores de tanda, y tres mas de Pinto, dos de Onofre y otras dos del Francés, á las cuales correspondió el *vicho* con gran fuerza.

Sonó el clarin y á peticion del público Lagartijo le clavó un par cuarteando en el embroque, no pudiendo hacer el vicho entrar al quiebro y otros dos mas dando el quiebro en uno de ellos con unánimes aplausos de el público que premia siempre todo lo que es bueno y vale.

Lo mató el Gordito despues de muchos pases innecesarios la mayor parte y por puro lujo, concluyendolo de dos pinchazos, una corta en direccion contraria, descabellandole al primer intento.

Salió el último de Lasaca, llamado *Merino*, negro azabache *cornicorto*, y huido.

Lo cojió Lagartijo con seis lances al *natural*.

Tomó cinco varas matando un caballo y lo banderilló el Gordito, poniéndole dos pares al quiebro uno bajo, otro delantero y medio por la izquierda en el brazuelo.

Se aomó Lagartijo de *trastos* y le hizo morder el polvo despues de varios pases de una buena hasta los *deos*.

En resúmen: los toros medianos, del propio modo los picadores: bien los banderilleros, señalándose el Cuco y Muñiz en inteligencia y bravura: los éspadas . . . silencio. La presidencia acertada: la entrada un lleno: murieron unos diez ciez caballos.

Barrabás y Calderilla.

www.ingramcontent.com/pod-product-compliance
Lightning Source LLC
Chambersburg PA
CBHW060541030726
47498CB00004B/1278